ITALY

HISTORY
AND
LANDSCAPE

ITALY

HISTORY
AND
LANDSCAPE

EUGENE BEER

BARNES
& NOBLE

NEW YORK

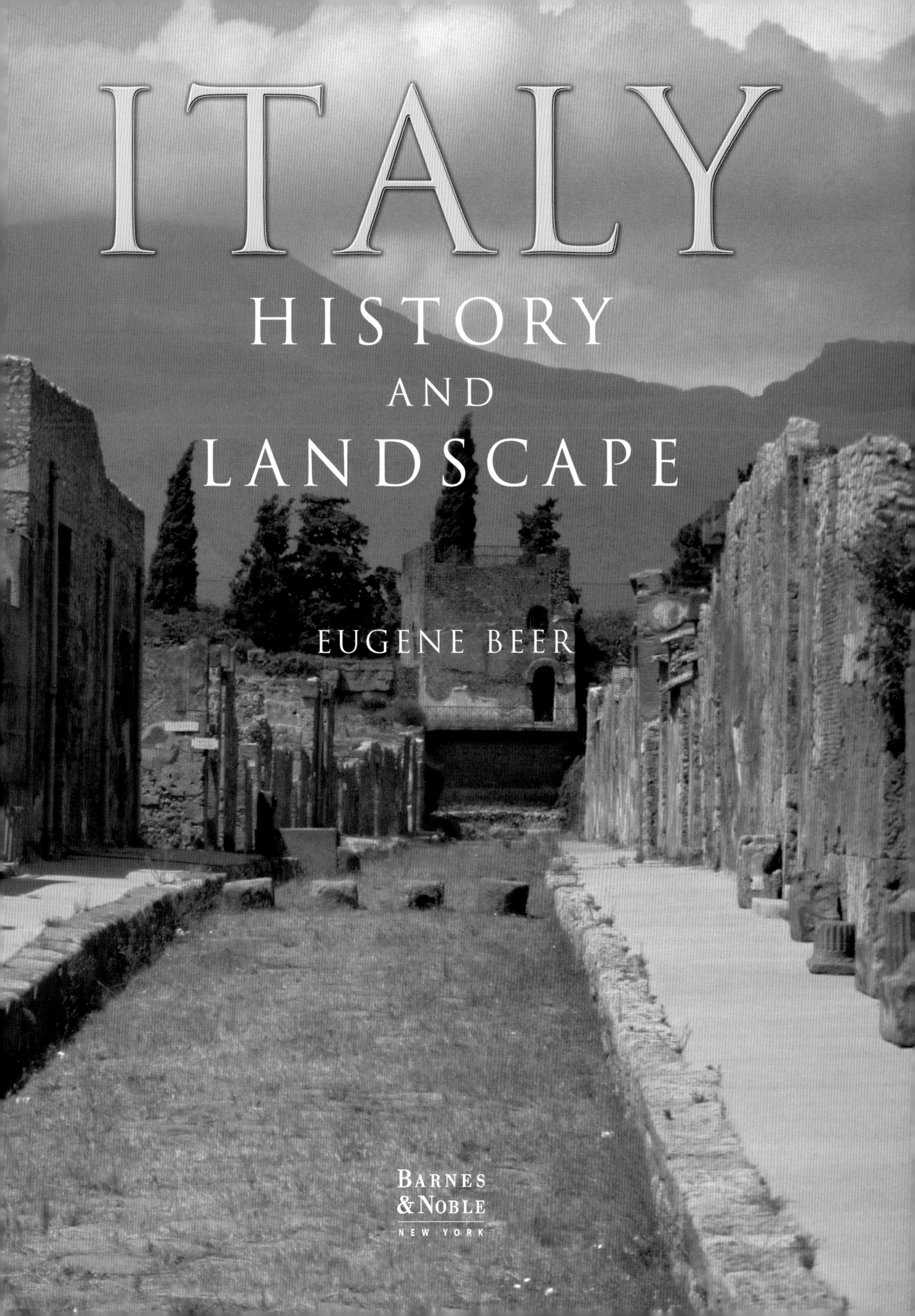

Editor: Don Gulbrandsen
Design: Danny Gillespie/Compendium Design

2006 Barnes & Noble Publishing

ISBN-13: 978-0-7607-8372-6
ISBN-10: 0-7607-8372-1

Printed and bound in China

1   3   5   7   9   10   8   6   4   2

For my friend Filippo Niciarelli

PAGE 1: Italy is a country with a rich history and archaeological treasures. These mosaics were unearthed during the excavations of Sybaris on the Gulf of Tarentum—a Greek city founded around 720 B.C. that was so luxurious it gave us the adjective "sybaritic."

PAGES 2–3: Of course, the best-known archaeological treasure trove in Italy is the area covered by Vesuvius's eruption in 79 A.D. This is the restored town of Pompeii, a World Heritage site.

RIGHT: Italy is not just ruins—the timeless countryside is always attractive, particularly in Tuscany.

PAGE 6: Sardinia is a beautiful island with unspoilt Mediterranean countryside—this is Tharros Beach.

CONTENTS

INTRODUCTION

INTRODUCTION

Italy has more UNESCO World Heritage Sites than any other country. Add stunning landscapes, superlative food and wine, and long months of sunshine and it is no wonder many tourists rate Italy as their favorite destination in the world.

For many people, Italy's main attraction is its scenery. Perhaps they cannot resist the photogenic Tuscan landscape of gently waving grasslands and tall cypress trees punctuating the skyline in such a perfect way that it looks as if an artist has painted it. Or it may be the silvery beauty of ancient olive trees, the yellow glow of a field of sunflowers, or the spectacular green of the sea off Sardinia. Others love the grand vistas, which means a visitor can take in several pretty medieval villages in a single glance. More adventurous souls who want to commune with nature's wonders

may head for the Dolomites in the far north. These incredible cathedrals of rock are arguably the most beautiful mountains in Europe, with ancient and unique geology that gives them a pink hue. Chic resorts such as Cortina d'Ampezzo offer world-class skiing, challenging hikes, and head-spinning mountaineering on rocks that dazzle the eyes with their daily iridescent light show.

Most visitors, however, are drawn by the sheer volume of history enclosed within this giant boot-shaped country sticking out into the Mediterranean. Thousands of years of migration, settlement, invasion, and empire have blessed the bel paese (beautiful country) with archeological remains, antiquities, architecture, and art that are second to none. Rome is the world's greatest open-air museum, with the Colosseum and St Peter's just a couple of examples of

its many treasures. Pompeii and Herculaneum are cities frozen in time by the ash and mud from Vesuvius, one of Italy's two active volcanoes. Sicily boasts wonderful, preserved Greek temples and Roman amphitheaters. Florence is home to Michelangelo's David. Siena hosts the annual great horse race, the Palio. Urbino is blessed with Renaissance treasures. Venice's watery magic makes it a magnet for romantics from around the world. The sleepy medieval hill towns were at one time some of the 400 rival city-states that held the reins of power in the fourteenth century. You can see, touch, and experience the past in Italy in such an intoxicating manner that the pull becomes irresistible and keeps bringing travelers back, time and time again.

Let's not forget Italian food and wine. Eating is a passion for Italians and they happily talk about food all the time. Commuters waiting for trains and buses while away the time discussing the finer points of a prosciutto they had as an antipasto or get into arguments about which type of pasta suits a particular sauce. Watch an Italian mamma in a butcher's shop and you will see how careful she is about having meat freshly minced or picking just the right size of pork chop. The same thing happens in a bakery—bread must be not too high, not too flat, and have just the right amount of well-cooked crust on top.

Italians are, by nature, a nation of foragers and they still collect wild lettuces, mushrooms, asparagus, and strawberries, venturing into the countryside in the early morning or making a day of it on a Sunday. Go to any town in Italy and you will see that every spare bit of land is taken up by vegetable plots whose owners proudly tend rows of artichokes, peas, broad beans, and tomatoes. Everything is bursting with flavor. A meal, therefore, whether it is in the finest restaurant or in the kitchens of ordinary families, starts and finishes with the question—what's in season? Simple, fresh food unfussily cooked is the key to Italian cooking and it's what sends millions of tourists into raptures.

BELOW: The beautiful Val di Funes in the Dolomites.

Italy is one of the world's biggest producers of wine, but for many years the wine had a very mixed reputation. A philosophy of quantity over quality dogged the industry and held it back while wines from France and the New World flourished. Over the last fifteen years, however, there has been a revolution in thinking. Thanks to visionaries like the Tuscan winemaker Piero Antinori, and the influx of young winemakers from countries such as Australia who bring with them the latest techniques, wines are being created that are unmistakably Italian but also have a new quality and freshness about them. Antinori's ervaro della Sala, from vineyards in Umbria, is taking on the great whites from Burgundy, for example. The huge Tuscan Reds like Sassacaia and Solaia command eye-watering prices in the world's top restaurants. If you can afford them, drink them! And if you can't, it's very satisfying to have a simple carafe of Italian homemade wine, served in a restaurant and probably made by the proprietor himself.

Italians have a built-in sense of style, and the country's fashion and furniture designers lead the way in their fields. Shopping, therefore, is another pleasure, whether it's in the high-fashion temples of Armani, Gucci, and Prada in cities like Rome or Milan or the small shop of a local tailor who crafts lovely, handmade men's shirts or beautifully tailored dresses. The country's tradition of artigiani—self-employed people who take great pride in their work—is highly valued and should be supported by visitors enthusiastically.

Italy has its problems, of course. This country of 58 million people has been struggling with a stagnant economy in recent years. The introduction of the euro as a monetary system has been highly problematic, causing a general rising of prices. Salaries, unfortunately, have not risen accordingly and many families struggle to make ends meet. Unemployment, under-investment in infrastructure, and inadequate funding for the arts trouble many modern Italians. Tourism remains the country's most valuable source of income and employment.

One leading Italian politician recently declared: "We are no longer a country of pizza, mandolins, and spaghetti". Of course not. Italy is a much more complex and modern society than that. But Italians are blessed to live in one of the most spectacular and culturally rich countries in the world. Visitors are lucky to be able to share in many of its pleasures.

RIGHT AND BELOW: Italy's remarkable architecture ensures it has more World Heritage sites than most countries. This is Sant'Antimo abbey church in Tuscany.

LEFT: Rome is the center of the Christian world and St. Peter's, in the Vatican City, is its largest church—60,000 can worship under its spectacular dome.

BELOW: Italy's riviera—the Ligurian coast—is studded with beautiful hilltop towns. This is San Bartolomeo al Mare, nestling between Imperia and Alassio.

ROME AND LAZIO

Tarquinia, once a major Etruscan city, lies in the hills of northern Lazio 50 miles north of Rome. A medieval town with views of the sea, Tarquinia would have been at the southern edge of the Etruscan Empire.

ROME AND LAZIO

Rome has been called the world's finest open-air museum, with nearly three thousand years of history jostling for space within a square mile. Every glance and every step gives visitors something new to absorb, and a good place to start is at the remains of the Circo Massimo, originally built by the Etruscans in the seventh century B.C. This is also where, in Roman times, chariot races entertained audiences of up to 300,000 people. Walk up the Palatine Hill, which is, legend has it, the site of the earliest settlement in the city. Here there are the ruins of imperial palaces that were homes to emperors from around A.D. 110 to 400, but there are also sixteenth-century gardens and a seventeenth-century pavilion.

Below the hill lies the Colosseum. Construction started in A.D. 72 and the grand opening eight years later saw 50,000 spectators enjoy a gruesome ten-day event that saw 50,000 animals killed. The Colosseum's life as an entertainment venue ended in the sixth century and for a thousand years or more Romans used its stone and marble as building materials for their new homes. Now, of course, it is one of Italy's top tourist attractions.

Just across the road from the Colosseum are the glorious ruins of the Roman Forum—the ancient center of government and business from 100 B.C. to A.D. 300. Just above the Forum is the extraordinary kitsch monument to Vittorio Emanuele, the first King of Italy after unification in 1861. It is nicknamed the "wedding cake" because of its extravagant appearance. The architects who created the giant white edifice held a celebratory lunch inside the belly of the giant statue of a horse, which stands in front of the monument, to mark is completion in 1911. Below is Palazzo Venezia, one of Rome's finest Renaissance buildings; it later became Italian dictator Benito Mussolini's office. The balcony at the front was where Il Duce spoke to huge crowds gathered in the piazza below.

Modern Rome has traffic and pollution like any other big city, but there are wonderful shops, restaurants, and bars—and there is good nightlife, too. Just wandering around this

ABOVE: Via Condotti, Rome's most famous shopping street, leads up to Piazza Spagna and the Spanish Steps—for centuries a meeting place for locals and visitors.

LEFT: The monument to Vittorio Emanuele II, Italy's first king after unification in 1870. Romans often refer to the outlandish structure as the "typewriter" or "wedding cake."

city filled with ancient monuments, medieval and Renaissance buildings, fountains and piazzas is a pleasure.

Visitors who venture outside Rome will find many rewards as well. Some twenty miles southeast of the city is Castel Gandolfo, one of several hill towns collectively known as the Castelli Romani. Overlooking Lake Albano, it is best known as the summer residence of the pope, but it is also popular with Romans who go there on weekends to breathe some fresh air, take a walk, and have lunch in a lakeside restaurant. There are also the attractive coastal resorts of Anzio and Nettuno, which have very good beaches. Tivoli, to the east, is the site of Villa D'Este and has beautiful gardens and the remains of Hadrian's villa. Beyond lie the Sabini Hills and the Abruzzi Mountains, which have excellent skiing in winter. The region of Lazio also has charming countryside, filled with vineyards and olive groves, as well as the lakes of Bracciano and Bolsena and classic walled towns like Viterbo and Amelia. The sixteenth-century Monster Park (Parco dei Mostri) in Bomarzo—the artist Salvador Dali called it his favorite place in the world—contains extraordinary monsters and fantasies carved out of tufo, the local rock.

LEFT: Throw a coin in the Trevi Fountain and make a wish that you will one day return to the Eternal City. Completed in 1762, the fountain has been a source of water since Roman times. Anita Ekberg famously frolicked in the water for Fellini's film *La Dolce Vita*.

PAGES 18–19: Gian Lorenzo Bernini's Fountain of the Four Rivers sits at the northern end of Piazza Navona—one of the favorite places for Romans to take their evening stroll or "passegiata." The figures at each edge represent the four corners of the earth.

BELOW: Mighty Neptune battles a giant octopus in the center of the Fontana dei Quattro Fiumi. Bernini, the fountain's creator, was one of seventeenth century Rome's principal architects and sculptors.

PAGES 22–23: Modern Rome is a city of almost three million people who live, work, play—and get stuck in traffic—in what was once the most powerful city on earth.

ABOVE: Lazio is a region often overlooked by visitors to Italy but it is an underestimated region full of ancient wonders such as the Ponte d'Abaddia.

RIGHT: The shadow of Michelangelo's giant dome moves towards the saints that watch over St. Peter's Square, which was designed by Bernini and built between 1656 and 1667. The piazza and the surrounding streets saw millions of people gather for the funeral of Pope John Paul II in April 2005.

PIVS · IX · P · M ·

LEFT: Dating from 1725, the Spanish Steps lead down from the beautiful Trinita dei Monti church to the Piazza Spagna below. Watch the sun set over the roofs of Rome or just watch the people rushing by. Especially popular among younger visitors to Rome, the steps are one of the essential places to see and be seen.

ABOVE: The arches and walls of the Colosseum were originally filled with statues and decorated with marble. Seating 50,000 spectators, the stadium allowed for occupation or evacuation in just ten minutes.

PAGES 26–27: The giant St. Peter's Basilica was officially completed in 1626. St. Peter was buried in a tomb on the site after his death in 64 A.D. and in 326 A.D. the first basilica was consecrated and stood for more than a thousand years. The new St. Peter's features the work by some of Italy's finest artists and architects including Bramante, Raphael, Peruzzi, and of course, Michelangelo.

PAGES 30–31: Originally built as a tomb for Emperor Hadrian in 135 A.D., Castel Sant'Angelo became a fortress to protect the Pope in the sixth century. A secret passage, the "passetto," that connects the Vatican to the castle, was built in the thirteenth century and popes could flee at times of peril to safety within the thick walls of the fortress.

LEFT: The spiral staircase within the Vatican Museum, whose extraordinary contents represent 500 years of Papal art collections and include of some of the world's most treasured art works. The Palace has more than 1,400 rooms and original places of worship including the Sistine Chapel with its miraculous ceiling by Michelangelo.

ABOVE: Trajan's Column was completed in 113 A.D. and is covered by a winding frieze that records the Emperor Trajan's conquests of Dacia (now Romania and Moldova). Standing 98 feet high, to the north of the Forum, the marble monument has an internal spiral staircase that leads to a platform at the top.

The stranded town of Civita di Bagnoregio in
Lazio. Surrounded by sharp-edged hills—
"calanchi"—the town has been connected to the
surrounding plateau by a man-made pedestrian
bridge since the original "tufo" rock ridge
collapsed.

VENICE AND
THE NORTHEAST

VENICE AND THE NORTHEAST

V enice is one of the most romantic cities on earth. Truman Capote wrote of it, "Venice is like eating an entire box of chocolate liqueurs at one go," and indeed, first-time visitors are usually stopped in their tracks when they first set eyes upon the unworldly scene of a city entirely built on water, with waves lapping up against doorsteps.

When Attila the Hun and the barbarians invaded in the fifth century, the region's fleeing refugees crossed the water to the marshy islands in the lagoon and turned them into a safe haven. Over the next thousand years the Venetians built 115 canals and more than 400 bridges to connect the 118 islands that make up Venice. As the city rose from the waters of the archipelago so did its wealth and power, becoming by the fifteenth and sixteenth centuries one of the most important merchant cities in the world. It was the headquarters of a trading empire that stretched to the Black Sea and included a sizeable chunk of the eastern edge of mainland Italy. As ever, pride comes before a fall and Venice fell into a very serious long-term decline after the sixteenth century.

The glories that are visible today are simply the remnants of what Venice must have been like at the height of its powers—but what glories they still are! St. Marks Square (Piazza San Marco), the very heart of Venice, is surrounded by the resplendent gold and gilt of Basilica di San Marco (St. Mark's Cathedral) and next door, the Doge's Palace (Palazzo Ducale), the center of power in Venice for more than a thousand years. The palace is a truly opulent expression of wealth through its elaborate marble facade and interior made up of priceless Renaissance art and dream-like decoration. At its rear is the Ponte dei Sospiri— the Bridge of Sighs—so called because of the sighs emitted by prisoners who had been condemned to death. This

PAGE 36–37: The huge seventeenth century church of Santa Maria della Salute dominates the entrance to the Grand Canal on the approach from St. Mark's Square. The Venetian authorities are considering replacing some of the millions of wooden posts on the banks of the canals with plastic ones that will be harder wearing than the original pine ones.

RIGHT: The main square in Marostica (Veneto) is Piazza Castello with its giant chess board paving. Human Chess—with the pieces played by actors in medieval costumes—is played in Septembers of years ending with an even number.

PAGES 40–41: The morning light has yet to catch the white and pink marble on the southwestern corner of the Doge's Palace at the southern end of St. Mark's Square. The winged lion on top of the column is the symbol of St. Mark.

bridge was where they had their last sight of the outside world. In front of the Doge's Palace is Venice's tallest structure, the 300-foot bell tower—Campanile di San Marco.

Today only 60,000 people live in Venice. Cars are forbidden and to get around people must travel on foot or by water. Venice's public transport system is based on the "vaporetti" waterbuses that shuttle up and down the main canals including the Grand Canal, which is the major artery of the city and has beautiful palaces on either side. There are twenty-six miles of canals, mostly narrow and dark as they thread through the buildings, crisscrossed by tiny bridges that link the thousands of tiny mysterious alleyways that slice through the city. Some 400 licensed gondoliers also operate here, hugely popular with tourists, of course.

The region outside Venice is mostly seen through a plane, train, or car window because everyone concentrates on the watery city. But to the north, west, and south are regions with much to offer.

Friuli-Venezia Giulia tucked away in the far northeastern corner of Italy remains one of its most undiscovered regions for non-Italian tourists. With its beautiful Adriatic beaches and islands, Alpine scenery, and the historic city of Trieste—"Vienna-By-The-Sea"—it is one of Italy's most versatile, cosmopolitan and rewarding places to visit.

The region also boasts one of the most beautiful cities in all of Italy—Verona—the legendary home of Romeo and Juliet with its amazing Roman arena that hosts spectacular open-air operas. Between Venice and Verona is Padua, where Galileo taught at its historic university and where Giotto created the beautiful frescoes in the Scrovegni Chapel.

Emilia Romagna is a region defined by the flat, sandy beaches of the Adriatic Riviera in the east and the imposing Apennines in the west. Renowned for its gastronomic pleasures—this is the home of Parma ham, Pamigiano Reggiano cheese, and Balsamic vinegar. Many of Italy's finest restaurants are in Bologna and eating here is one of the delights of any trip to Italy. The city is also home to the oldest University in Italy (established 1088) as well as to outstanding medieval piazzas and porticos.

LEFT: Cittadella, to the north of Padova, was built in 1220 as part of the Padovan city state. A ring of protective walls still encircle the town and the area was once a virtual retirement zone for Roman soldiers who were given square fields to farm as reward for loyal service.

PAGES 44–45: The tiny fishing village of Burano, in the lagoon to the northeast of Venice, is a colorful center of traditional lace making.

LEFT: The busy fishing port of Chioggia, at the southern end of the Venetian Lagoon, is a ninety-minute boat ride from Venice's Lido. Often described as a smaller, quieter version of Venice, Chioggia is a charming alternative.

PAGES 48–49: Il Castello (The Castle) near Valbona is a thirteenth-century castle that in 1635 came into the possession of the Cornaro family, who at one time were the occupants of dozens of grand villas in the Veneto region.

ABOVE AND RIGHT: Italian architecture is all about columns—in particular the classical orders of Doric (as seen on the Parthenon and at right), Ionic, and Corinthian. In Venice and the Veneto the best-known proponent of the Classical style was Andrea Palladio (1508–1580) whose style would sweep across Europe and influence Inigo Jones and Sir Christopher Wren.

ABOVE: Bassano del Grappa is home to this
fascinating astrological clock in the Piazza Liberta.
The clock mechanism, installed in 1743 by
Bartolomeo Ferranci, still works.

RIGHT: Statue by Orazio Marinali of St. Bassiano, the
patron saint of Bassano del Grappa, that stands in the
central Piazza Liberta. Marinali (1643–1720) is
considered the greatest seventeenth-century Veneto
sculptor.

LEFT: The nineteenth century poet Robert Browning lived at number 153 on what is now Via Robert Browning in the little town of Asolo in the foothills of the Dolomites. Known as the town of a "hundred horizons," Asolo is regarded as the most beautiful of Veneto's small towns.

ABOVE: The basilica in Aquileia, just west of Trieste in Friuli Venezia Giulia. Aquileia was one of the most important cities in the Roman Empire and the Basilica was originally built in 313 A.D. The floor of the basilica is covered by one of the world's most precious Christian mosaics dating from the fourth century. The floor is protected by thick glass raised three foot above the mosaic.

LEFT: Treviso, despite being in the foothills of the Alps, is laced by tiny canals that run through the center of this charming medieval town. It is also home to the Benetton clothing brand.

ABOVE: Palladio's sixteenth century church on the island of San Giorgio Maggiore can be seen in the distance through the arches of the Doge's Palace in Venice.

LEFT: A colorful balcony on the island of Burano in the Venice Lagoon. For most Italians the tiny balconies outside their apartments are the nearest they get to having a garden.

RIGHT: The beautifully preserved medieval city of Montagnana, 30 miles south west of Padova, shows off its subtle pastel shades.

ABOVE: Nestling in the foothills of the pre-Alps, Follina's churches and abbeys display their cistercian and eastern influences. The town is at the very north of the "Prosecco Route"—the land of vines that produce Veneto's famous sparkling wines.

RIGHT: Villa Barbaro, in Treviso, is another of Palladio's designs. It was built around 1560 and has all the hallmarks of his Classical concepts—columns supporting a pediment with a frieze above the facade.

PAGES 62–63
Still in use today, Palladio's Teatro Olimpico reproduces the outdoor theaters of Greece. Finished after his death in 1580 by his student Vincento Seamozzi it is Europe's oldest indoor theater.

GENIO
THEATRVM HOC
EREXIT
LLADIO   ARCHIT.

ABOVE: Originally built in the fourteenth century over the River Adige that cuts through the city, Verona's Ponte Scaligero was destroyed during the Second World War. The remains of the bridge were salvaged as much as possible and used in its restoration.

RIGHT: The sculptor Antonio Canova was born in the village of Possagno in 1757. After he died, in 1822, his heart was placed in a marble pyramid he had designed for Titian in the church of Santa Maria Gloriosa dei Frari in Venice, and the rest of his remains in a temple in Possagno.

PAGES 66–67: The tiny village has a museum dedicated to the prodigious artist—Il Museo Canoviano di Possagno.

BELOW: Michelangelo and Palladio entered the competition to design a new stone bridge that would cross the Grand Canal. In the end the winner was Antonio da Ponte and his design for the Ponte de Rialto has become one of the most iconic of Venice's architectural sights.

RIGHT: Palladio's church of San Giorgio Maggiore sits on its own island in the Venice Lagoon. Inside are two masterpieces by Tintoretto, *The Last Supper* and *Gathering of Manna*.

ABOVE: The iron "head" of a gondola was originally designed to give a gondola longitudinal stability, helping to balance the weight of the gondolier against the unequal pitch of the craft itself. A gondola is asymmetric—its left side being 9½ inches wider than the right.

RIGHT: The sixteenth century frescoes on Casa Mazzanti in Verona's Piazza della Erbe are typical of the elegant artworks found in the historic home of Romeo and Juliet. The Piazza, with its busy market and fine Renaissance palaces, is Verona's place to meet and is in every respect the city's hub.

PAGES 72–73: It is just about two miles long, but over 200 palaces can be seen along the water's edge of Venice's Grand Canal. At night the "Canalazzo" is one of the most beautiful sights in the world.

LEFT: The little Island of Torcello was the original landing place in the lagoon for the fleeing Venetians. They built their first cathedral, Santa Maria Assunta, in the eleventh century and by the sixteenth century the island had ten churches and a population of 20,000.

RIGHT: The Palazzo Querini-Stampalia gives a flavor of what life must have been like at the height of Venetian power. Now a museum, its 20 rooms show off the art and furnishings of one of eighteenth century Venice's most affluent families.

BELOW: The facade of the Doge's Palace was designed by Giovanni Buon and built between 1309 and 1424. It is nearly 500 feet long. The third story was rebuilt after a sixteenth-century fire.

PAGES 76–77: Gondolas at rest under the early morning mist in the Lagoon off St. Mark's Square. The views of Venice from the bell tower or "campanile" of San Giorgio Maggiore across the water are some of the best in the city.

PAGES 80–81: The Rialto Bridge on Venice's Grand Canal was originally a fragile wooden structure that straddled the water from the thirteenth century until the construction of Antonio da Ponte's extravagant single-arch replacement in 1592.

ABOVE AND RIGHT: Possibly the most photographed form of transportation in the world. Each gondola is made from eight different types of wood forming 280 separate parts. They can be 36 feet long and weigh 1,300 pounds but seem to glide effortlessly through the water in the hands of a skilled gondolier and just one very long oar.

LEFT AND RIGHT: Venice's 60,000 residents live in buildings supported by millions of long wooden poles buried in the mud below the water. Subsidence has become a major problem in recent years and a spate of very low tides allows air into the foundations which causes rotting of the ancient wooden pilings.

LEFT: Venice's gondoliers take great pride in personalizing their unique craft with ornate decorations and personal emblems. There are only 400 licensed gondoliers but no women—so far.

ABOVE: Every year, for the 10 days running up to Shrove Tuesday, Venetians come out to play in mysterious masks for their historic "carnevale." For centuries the carnival lasted for several weeks and was an excuse for all sorts of licentious and bacchanalian behavior. Now it is a far more commercial affair drawing visitors to the city at an otherwise inclement time of year.

RIGHT: The head or "pettini" of a Gondola by tradition represents the six quarters or "sestieri" that the city of Venice is divided into.

ABOVE: Is there a more romantic way to arrive at a hotel than by boat? Many of Venice's hotels have their own landing stages and it is possible to land at Venice's Marco Polo airport and journey to your hotel by water taxi.

RIGHT: A one-bedroom apartment in a restored "palazzo" on the Grand Canal would set you back $2,000,000 should you be interested. They are some of the most desired properties in the world.

LEFT: The Campanile in St. Mark's Square is the tallest building in Venice and has stunning views of the city and the lagoon. On very clear days the Dolomites can be seen in the far distance.

PAGES 90–91: The fastest forms of transport along the canals are the licensed motorboats that residents use for commuting or visiting friends and local traders employ for everyday deliveries. Up until 1846, when the rail and road link to the mainland was built, everything that Venice needed had to be brought in by boat.

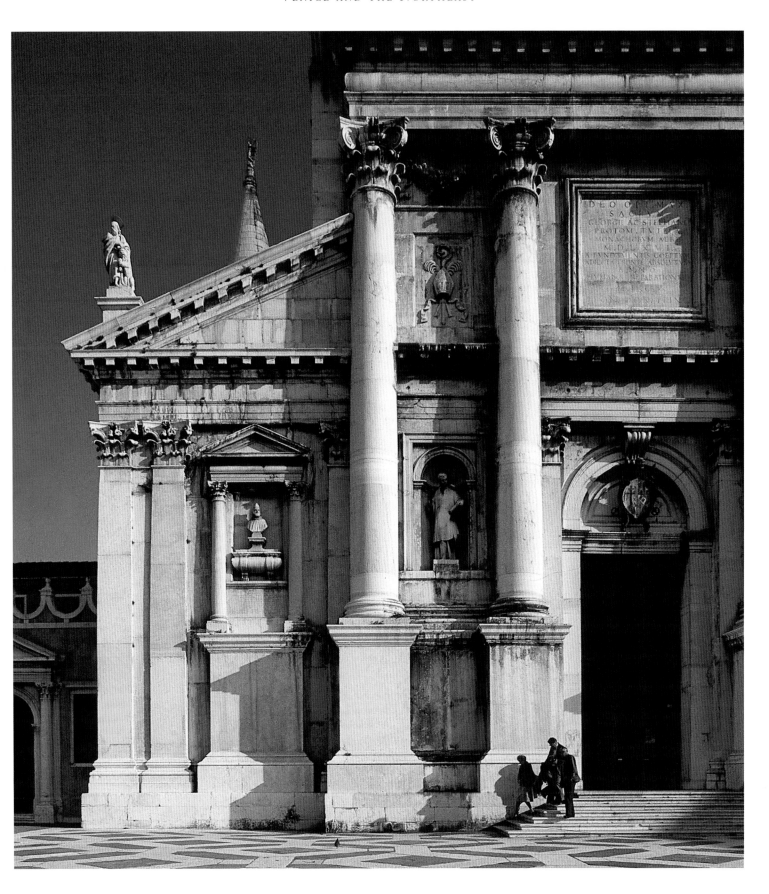

LEFT: The church of Santi Apostoli is on Venice's Campo dei Santi Apostoli, a general meeting point and crossroads.

ABOVE AND PAGE 94: The Basilica di San Marco was originally finished in 1094 and was designed to house the body of Venice's patron Saint, St. Mark that had been stolen by the Venetians from Alexandria nearly 300 years before. Nine centuries of constant embellishment has resulted in its extraordinarily exotic appearance with overtones of Romanesque, Islamic, Byzantine, and European architecture.

PAGE 95: San Giorgio Maggiore is just one of hundreds of islands in Venice Lagoon that were made habitable by the original Venetians fleeing from the Barbarian invasion of the mainland.

DEO · OPT · MAX · VNI · AC · TRINO

PAGES 96–97: The island of Giudecca, to the south of Venice, is home to the great architect Palladio's majestic church Il Redentore. Built in the sixteenth century to mark the end of a great plague the best views of it are from across the water. The island of Giudecca is also home to Venice's most famous hotel—the Cipriani.

LEFT: Antonio Canova designed Possagno's humble "parish church" himself. The famous sculptor set the Tempi di Canoviano Possagno on a series of hillocks at the foot of the Monfenera and Tomba hills.

ABOVE: Built in 1542 and designed by Palladio, the impressive Villa Godi-Malinverni in the Province of Vicenza boasts frescoes by Zelotti, Padovan, and Battista del Moro.

LEFT: The Lido is the island playground for Venetians and tourists. Eight miles long, the island acts as a barrier between the Lagoon and the Adriatic. A popular destination for writers such as Byron and Thomas Mann, the Lido's beach and huts featured memorably in the film of the latter's novel *Death in Venice*.

ABOVE: The church of Santa Maria della Salute was built after the Venetian senate had promised God that they would build it if he spared more lives from the plague that had killed a third of Venice's 150,000 inhabitants in late 1630.

FLORENCE AND TUSCANY

FLORENCE AND TUSCANY

Gently rolling landscapes dotted with cypress trees, breathtakingly pretty medieval hilltop towns, museums and galleries crammed with artistic treasures and, of course, wine and food to die for—Tuscany remains the jewel in Italy's crown, the most visited and most popular region of the country.

Three thousand years ago, Tuscany was the center of Etruscan civilization. These highly artistic and organized people established towns and cities such as Arezzo, Chiusi, Cortona, and Volterra that still exist today. They were part of the Etruscan League, a self-governing group of cities that formed the basis of the early Etruscan empire. Although coexisting, they were also immensely competitive, sparking constant battles and feuding, which continued until the fifth century, when the mighty Romans moved north and conquered the territory.

The creative influence of the Etruscans remained, however, and their tradition of enterprise and art makes it no accident that Tuscany was the birthplace of the Renaissance. Working in Florence—the heart of both Tuscany and the movement—Leonardo da Vinci painted his Annunciation, Botticelli left the world his Birth of Venus, and Michaelangelo sculpted David. Florence was home to the powerful Medici dynasty that besides producing three popes, sponsored of many of the artists of the Renaissance. The fruits of their patronage can be seen in

the Uffizi (home to Botticelli's Birth of Venus), Accademia (Michaelangelo's David), Pitti Palace (once home to the Medicis, it now displays masterpieces by Raphael, Rubens, Titian, and Caravaggio to name a few), the Duomo, and in dozens of towns and cities across the region.

Tuscany is perhaps most people's favorite image of Italy: Stunning landscapes, perfect medieval towns, and museums and galleries crammed with artistic treasures; wonderful food, classic wines, and bright green peppery olive oil; sleepy hill towns basking baking under the white-hot summer sun with their narrow shady streets; undulating velvet hills, punctuated by the iconic darkest green cypress trees, that legend has it, show the spirits the way to heaven. Tuscany is a land that has been "touched by the genius of man and nature." Movies such as A Room with a View, The English Patient, and Under the Tuscan Sun have used the beautiful Tuscan landscape and architecture as the most elegant and dramatic backdrop. No visit to Italy should be complete without feasting upon the delights of Florence or Siena or their smaller architecturally stunning neighbors of Pienza, Montalcino, or Lucca.

The food, wine, and oil of Tuscany are legendary. Less well known are the fantastic meats that Tuscans enjoy so heartily. The massive bistecca alla fiorentina is one of the most popular dishes and always washed down with a hearty Tuscan red.

Tuscany, like its art and gastronomy, is at one and the same time gentle and dramatic: Picture-perfect views of precariously perched historic hill towns looming high over rolling fields of poppies or sunflowers; 120 protected nature preserves; piping-hot thermal springs fed by volcanic fissures; fiery olive oil that Tuscans claim is the best in Italy; the giant Brunello wines of Montalcino; and the crumbly Pecorino cheese made from the milk of their small flocks of sheep. Tuscany is a feast for all the senses.

PAGES 102–103: A typical Tuscan scene of poppies and wild flowers line an old track leading to the 12th century monastery of Sant 'Antimo which sits peacefully beneath the old hill town of Castelnuovo dell'Abate.

LEFT: A crossing point in Florence over the River Arno from Roman times, the Ponte Vecchio was built in 1345. The bridge is crammed with jewelry stores on each side and must be one of the busiest pedestrian bridges in the world.

PAGES 106–107: Thanks to the patronage of the powerful Medici family the Uffizi Gallery contains many of the most famous paintings from the Renaissance. The Uffizi Palace was originally designed in 1560 to be the offices, "uffizi," of Cosimo, a self appointed Grand Duke of Tuscany. After his death, in 1574, the family placed their vast collection of art within the building. Some of the greatest works by Uccello, Giotto, Lippi, Caravaggio, Raphael, Michelangelo, Rembrandt, Titian, and da Vinci are on display on the top floors of the palace. Visible, at the end of the street, is the bell tower (campanile) of the Piazza della Signoria, the bell of which was used, at times of threat to Florence, as a call to arms to its citizens.

RIGHT: Sitting 1,700 feet high above sparse and forbidding countryside, Volterra is an ancient city with fine Etruscan and Roman antiquities. The unfinished Duomo sits in a picture perfect medieval piazza and contains a superb fifteenth century fresco by Benozzo Gozzoli.

Pages 110–111: Massa Marittima, in Tuscany's Maremma, was an important independent city state with rich mineral mines in the thirteenth century. These closed at the end of the fourteenth century leaving the town impoverished and untouched for over 500 years. The cathedral is one of Tuscany's finest.

RIGHT: Montepulciano, famous for its robust red wines, perches high above the plains to its east, 2,000 feet above sea level. The approach to the center of the town is steep but worth it. Medieval alleys with charming cafes and shops lead to the glorious Piazza Grande and its unfinished Duomo. Antonio da Sangallo, one of the town's architects, designed the lovely church of San Biagio that sits just below Montepulciano itself.

PAGES 114–115: The church of Santa Croce dates from 1228 when Franciscans, who had arrived in Florence some years before, built the original. The resting place of some of the most famous Renaissance figures including Michelangelo, Machiavelli, and Galileo Galilei, the church also contains frescoes by Giotto.

ABOVE: One of the joys of Florence is to wander the tiny streets off the main thoroughfares and discover the many old shops selling the work of the city's traditional artisans, sometimes with a contemporary touch.

RIGHT: The Medici family did nothing by halves. When the family decided they wanted their own church they commissioned Brunelleschi to design it and fortunes were lavished on the structure called San Lorenzo. Construction was completed in 1469.

PAGE 118-119: The Museum of Palazzo Davanzati is also known as the Museum of the Traditional Florentine House. Originally a fourteenth century nobleman's house, it became a state museum in 1951. The many rooms of the Palazzo Davanzati contain furnishings, paintings and objects from all over Florence and faithfully capture the interior of a typical Florence house at the time of the Renaissance.

PAGES 120–121: The River Arno flows westward through the center of Florence and normally has a glass like appearance. 1n November 1966 the Arno rose to a height of nearly 20 feet and flooded the center of the city killing 39 people as well as wrecking tens of thousands of homes and businesses and causing terrible damage to the city's art and treasures.

PAGE 122: The tower (campanile) of the thirteenth century Palazza della Signoria (Palazzo Vecchio). The bell was used, at times of threat to Florence, as a signal for its citizens to take up arms and be ready to defend the city.

PAGE 123: Brunelleschi's ingenious dome for Florence's Duomo is best seen from a distance in order to appreciate its brilliance. The architect was so intent on completing the dome, in record time, that he built a worker's canteen between the inner and outer dome so that lunches could be taken atop the construction avoiding time wasting trips down to the ground. Work started on the dome in 1420 and was completed in 1436.

LEFT: Walking through Florence at night gives the visitor a glimpse of what the city must have been like in the heyday of the eighteenth century Grand Tour.

RIGHT: The entrance hall and inner staircase of the Palazzo Davanzati show the original fourteenth century stone work complete with interior drainpipes.

PAGES 126–127: Etruscans called Pitigliano "The Eagle's Nest" due to its position on steep volcanic "tufo." The town is crammed with cellars, caves, and Etruscan tombs that form a honeycomb in the rock below. The aqueduct, in the foreground, was built in 1545.

LEFT: Lucca's twelfth century Duomo of San Martino is dwarfed by the Lombard bell tower that sits at its side. Nicola Pisano and Giudetto da Como contributed to the cathedral's main portal and facade.

ABOVE: This tiny chapel, with cypress trees standing guard, is not far from Pienza on the way to San Quirico d'Orcia. Postcards of this most Tuscan scene can be found everywhere in the region.

PAGES 130–131: The Val d'Orcia became a UNESCO World Heritage site in 2004 because of its "distinctive aesthetics" and inspiration to artists over many centuries. It is perhaps the most quintessentially perfect part of Tuscany.

PAGES 132–133: The lights of the Ponte Vecchio and the Lungarno Acciaiuoli reflected in the waters of the River Arno in Florence. The northern bank of the Arno has many of the most famous hotels, cafes, and bars of Florence including an outpost of Venice's legendary Harry's Bar.

LEFT: One of Lucca's many tranquil piazzas. Lucca is completely encircled by giant, hollow walls, topped by a wide flat path that is ideal for a leisurely stroll or cycle ride. Most of Lucca is completely traffic free which makes it one of the most pleasant of cities to explore.

PAGES 136–137: Many farmhouses in Tuscany remain frustratingly empty. This beautiful example near Pienza has probably fallen victim to Italy's inheritance laws which divide ownership between many living relatives, making a decision to sell or rebuild anything but straightforward.

PAGES 138–139: The thick walls of Monteriggioni and its fourteen towers were built by Siena in the thirteenth century as a northern defense against their northern arch enemy—Florence. It is visible for miles around, and was immortalized by Dante who pictured it full of terrible giants in his *Divine Comedy.*

BELOW: The Val d'Orcia covered by the dawn mist as seen from the walls of Pienza. Pope Pius II commissioned the design of Pienza, after whom it was named, in the fifteenth century and it is now famous for its cheese made from sheep's milk—Pecorino di Pienza.

PAGE 140: Tuscany's beauty is so extreme that its landscape is often described as having been designed by the hand of a giant divine artist. The perfection of this cypress-lined road near Monticello makes the legend easy to believe.

PAGE 141: The remains of the Gothic Abbey of San Galgano lie forlornly in fields to the south of Siena. This old Cistercian abbey fell prey to a succession of exploitative abbots who thought nothing of stripping it bare until, by 1548, even the lead from the roof was gone, leaving its eventual collapse inevitable.

PAGES 144–145: Every year, at the end of April and beginning of May, millions of pure red poppies cover the fields of Tuscany and the landscape is transformed for a few short weeks.

LEFT: San Gimignano has one of Italy's most distinctive skylines with thirteen tall towers rising above the town. At the height of its wealth there were 72 towers, perhaps giving rise to its nickname of "Tuscany's Medieval Manhattan." The Collegiata's plain twin towers belie its elaborate interior.

BELOW: Work on the elaborate facade of Siena's Duomo began in 1226 with further additions by Pisano between 1284 and 1296. Inside is the Piccolomini altar with four statues of saints carved by a young Michelangelo.

PAGES 148–149: The twelfth century abbey of Sant'Antimo, six miles south of Montalcino, where Cistercian Monks perform mass on a Sunday morning accompanied by Gregorian chants.

PAGES 150–151: Acclaimed director Anthony Minghella used the rolling Tuscan landscape of the Val d'Orcia to great effect as a location for the Oscar winning movie *The English Patient*.

BELOW: Siena's Duomo and striking Campanile loom over the city. There were plans for the Duomo to be even bigger but after plague hit the city in 1348 work on an extension was abandoned.

PAGE 154–155: Dusk falls over the Baptistery, Duomo, and Campanile in Florence. Michelangelo described the doors on the eastern side of the Baptistery as "so beautiful they are worthy to be the Gates of Paradise." The Baptistery dates from the sixth century, the Duomo from the thirteenth with its scene stealing dome and the Campanile, by Giotto, from the fourteenth.

BELOW: This view of Siena's Duomo and Campanile only comes after climbing the 503 steep steps of the 336-foot Torre del Mangia in the Piazza del Campo. It is Italy's tallest medieval tower and was completed in 1348.

ABOVE: Siena's Duomo was completed in 1263 and some of the statues on the lower facade were created by master artist Giovanni Pisano from 1285. The upper half of the facade was finished in the fourteenth century with further mosaics added in the nineteenth century.

RIGHT: The Fonte Gaia was built between 1408 and 1419 and designed by Jacopo della Quercia. The fountain is at the end of Siena's 18-mile network of water tunnels, aqueducts, and wells. Most of the fountain is now a replica with the original eroded panels removed for safe keeping.

PAGES 160–161: Siena's Campo ("field") sits on the site of an old Roman Forum and its shell like shape was first paved in the twelfth century. The white lines divide the paving into nine parts and represent the city's original medieval ruling body of nine.

LEFT: The intricate facade of San Michele in Foro, Lucca. Work began on the church in 1143 and they completed the facade before money ran out to complete the project. The main body of the church finishes below the upper level of the front of the church, creating a disconcerting effect with arches and windows left hanging in the air.

ABOVE: The church of San Biagio, Montepulciano, is considered to be the architect Antonio da Sangallo the Elder's greatest work. He was already busy reworking many of Montepulciano's existing buildings when he was commissioned, in 1518, to design a church for pilgrims on the hill below the town.

ABOVE: Pisa's Piazza del Duomo is also known as the Campo dei Miracoli—Field of Miracles. It is best known as the site of the Leaning Tower of Pisa. This was only ever intended to be the bell tower for the beautiful Duomo and Baptistery that dominate the piazza. Most people visit Pisa for the Tower but the Duomo, begun in 1063, with its shining white marble and its Baptistery are actually more interesting. The "lean" of the Tower was finally halted in 2001.

RIGHT AND ABOVE RIGHT: The Palio is a colorful and dramatic event that has taken place since medieval times in Siena's Piazza del Campo—main square. Siena was, for centuries, Florence's main rival for power and is made up of seventeen fiercely competitive districts, called "contrade." These compete, in July and August every year, in the legendary Palio—the 90-second horse race round the Campo in Siena's center.

MILAN, LOMBARDY AND THE ALPS

MILAN, LOMBARDY, AND THE ALPS

Milan, the business and fashion capital of Italy, the magnificent lakes of Como and Garda, and the Renaissance cities of Pavia, Cremona, and Mantova, sum up this northern region of Italy, which sits in the main part of the Po Valley and borders Switzerland.

With its stylish shops, restaurants, and cafes, contemporary Milan nevertheless sits comfortably alongside historic Milan, filled with Gothic splendors and art and buildings that would make Florence and Rome proud. The center of the city is dominated by one of the world's most amazing cathedrals. Milan's Duomo, which can hold a congregation of 40,000, was started in 1386 and the last gate was only completed in 1965. It sits in its own piazza with all the major streets of Milan leading to and from it. The Galleria Vittorio Emanuele, possibly the world's oldest shopping mall, runs from the Piazza del Duomo to the opera house of La Scala and is a great place to settle down with a cappuccino and watch the world go by, especially if the northern winds are blowing outside.

The recently refurbished La Scala, built in 1778, is probably the most famous opera house in the world and still puts on thrilling performances every season. This is where Verdi cut his musical teeth, where Maria Callas sang her way into legend, and where every aspiring conductor or singer dreams of performing. The theater houses a museum containing original scores by Verdi and Toscanini.

One of the world's greatest art treasures, Leonardo da Vinci's *The Last Supper,* occupies a large part of a wall in the monastery of Santa Marie delle Grazie, on the west side of Milan. Painted between 1495 and 1498, this masterpiece has survived being painted over, bombed, and having a door built where Jesus' feet should be. It has become an even bigger attraction because of the book *The Da Vinci Code* and there are often lines of people waiting to see it. Subject to almost never-ending restoration, the painting's vivid colors and emotional intensity still inspire awe.

In the far northern part of Lombardy, bordering Switzerland, lies the beautiful area of Valtellina with its magnificent Alpine scenery. Lake Como is one of Europe's deepest and was once an essential stopping-off point for rich travelers in the eighteenth and nineteenth centuries. Modernization has dulled its charms a little but there are still opulent villas and gorgeous gardens bordering the lake and many visitors. Lake Garda, with its mirror-like surface that in the summer makes it a target for water sports enthusiasts, is similarly impressive and visitors head for lakeside resorts such as Limone sul Garda and Desenzano to soak up the scenery from cafes and bars.

South of Milan, the towns of Pavia, Cremona, and Mantova lie in the heart of the river Po's floodplain. Pavia was once one of the north's great cities and the first Duke of Milan, Galeazzo Visconti III, ordered the shipping of hundreds of tons of finest Carrara marble to build the Certosa monastery in 1396. This extraordinary edifice remains a huge tourist attraction, and is one of the most decorated and elaborate facades of any religious structure in Italy. Cremona,

to the east, is the place to buy a violin—or just to watch one being made—thanks to the talented artisans who continue the work of Antonio Stradivari, who set up shop here in 1680. Mantova is another of Italy's fine medieval cities. Originally surrounded—for protection from its enemies—by manmade lakes on all sides, it was recently voted "the most livable city in Italy."

PAGES 166–167: Milan's Piazza del Duomo and its magnificent Gothic Cathedral at Christmas. Construction began on the Duomo in 1386 and was completed, depending upon who you believe, in 1897 or 1965.

BELOW LEFT: Lake Como, in the north of Lombardy just below Switzerland, is edged by lush scenery, beautiful villages, elegant villas, and glorious mountains.

RIGHT: Parma is one of Italy's most prosperous towns and home to its eponymous ham and Parmiggiano cheese. Its eleventh century Duomo (competed in 1534) is a superb example of Lombard-Romanesque architecture.

PAGES 170–171: An elevator is available to take visitors to the roof of the Duomo. Here one can walk through the statues and pinnacles and, on the clearest of days, catch sight of the Swiss Alps and the Matterhorn 50 miles away.

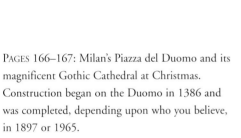

ABOVE: Art-glass window in Milan's Duomo.

RIGHT: The northern side of Milan's Duomo shows off some of its decoration. Only St Peter's in Rome and Spain's Seville Cathedral are bigger. It remains Italy's biggest and finest Gothic building.

LEFT: Leonardo da Vinci's *The Last Supper* occupies a large part of a wall in the monastery of Santa Marie delle Grazie, pictured here, on the west side of Milan.

PAGES 176–177: Bellagio, on the shore of Lake Como, is thought by some to be Europe's prettiest village. With idyllic cobbled streets and beautiful gardens, Bellagio is the jewel in Lake Como's crown.

PAGES 178–179: Lombardy's lakes are famous for their elegant eighteenth and nineteenth century shoreside villas whose elegant formal gardens have commanding views over the icy waters below—these belong to Villa Carlotta. Como, with a depth of over 1,300 feet, is Europe's deepest lake.

ABOVE: The many statues in the Baroque Garden of Palazzo Borromeo were added in the latter half of the seventeenth century and are meant to symbolize the forces of nature.

RIGHT: The Castello Sforzesco was built by Francesco Sforza, the fourth Duke of Milan. A heroic soldier, or mercenary, Sforza's creation is now a museum with an eclectic collection of antiquities and art. Michelangelo's last work, the unfinished Rondanini Pieta, is found in the Salle delle Asse gallery within the castle.

PAGES 182–183: A sunny day beside Lake Como is one of the most idyllic ways of passing the time. Known locally as Lago Di Como, it is made up of three long converging lakes beside which the small towns of Bellaggio, Tremezzo, Menaggio, and Varenna sit.

PAGES 184–185: Another view of Bellagio on Lake Como. Even on a dull day the beauty of the lakes of Northern Lombardy are still breath taking. The magnificent waterside villas are surrounded with formal gardens that were designed to give the wealthy owners enchanting views of the waters below.

LEFT: The hermitage of Santa Caterina del Sasso, to the south of Laverno on Lake Maggiore, was built in the twefth century as a tribute to God for sparing the life of a local man from a storm on the lake.

BOLZANO AND THE DOLOMITES

BOLZANO AND THE DOLOMITES

Alto Adige, the northernmost and least Italian of all Italy's regions, is a land of majestic mountains, castles, glaciers, and nature reserves that are the last refuge of Alpine brown bears. The amazing geography is a magnet for mountaineers, skiers, hikers, and nature and wildlife enthusiasts from all over the world. The acclaimed French Architect Le Corbusier described the Dolomites as "the most beautiful work of architecture in the world." Reckoned by many to be the most beautiful mountains in Europe, the Dolomites are, compared to other Alpine areas, pristine. With summits of almost 11,000 feet, it is the geology of the thirty-plus massifs that make up the

Dolomites unique. Composed of a kind of ancient magnesium limestone coral—the rock was named after the French geologist Dolomieu—these giant reefs have been sculpted over millions of years by the elements to produce a unique range of shapes and colors. Jagged sheer pinnacles, sawtoothed ridges, and cathedral-like spires take on ethereal hues as the light of the day and night changes. The mineral composition of the rocks that form the Dolomites means that the mountains themselves hold onto and gradually change their color. The most spectacular time is at dusk, when the "enrosadira" occurs; bright red flashes of light seem to come out of the rocks and for a minute or two

nature stages a glorious light show. During the long winter nights the peaks put on yet another show, remaining luminous throughout the night.

Also known as the South Tirol, Alto Adige borders Austria in the north and Switzerland to the west. It became part of Italy after the World War I when the victorious allies broke up the Austro-Hungarian Empire. Still mainly German speaking, the region is a true cultural crossroads—dual language road signs point the way. This is where gutten tag meets buon giorno. The distinctly Germanic cuisine—more wiener schnitzel than vitello—is eaten alongside Italian staples and the region has its own political party and mainly German language media. Underlining the cultural difference of the Dolomites are the Ladin people, who live in the beautiful Val Gardena area, between Bolzano and Cortina d'Ampezzo, and speak an ancient and impenetrable language that blends ancient Latin with various Celtic dialects. The Ladin people are descendants of an ancient civilization that inhabited the main parts of the Alps of Switzerland, Austria, and Italy.

Bolzano (or Bozen), the capital of the region, is chic and completely bilingual, and the Museum of Archeology houses the remarkable remains of "Oetzi"—the 5,000-year-old "Iceman" who was found lying in a glacier on the Italian border with Austria. Bolzano is one of Italy's most desirable places to live in, with wonderful Tyrolean style churches and monuments as well as colorful markets and a thriving café culture and nightlife.

PAGES 188–189 AND BELOW: The hills and mountains of the Dolomites appeal to visitors all year round. Spring and fall (pictured) are particularly popular times due to the lush changing colors of the seasons.

ABOVE: View over hay stooks and down the Val di Funes towards the Odle mountains in the Dolomite range. This region is renowned for its hearty food and drink which is needed to keep out the cold in winter.

RIGHT: The onion shaped domes on churches in the Dolomites are strong reminders of the region's links with the old Austro-Hungarian Empire and Eastern European-style architecture.

LEFT: Trieste's Museum of the Sea reflects the connection between this old city and its position as the "Gateway to the South and East" in terms of trade from Europe. An important port of the Austro-Hungarian Empire, it lives up to its nickname of "Vienna-by-the-Sea."

ABOVE: Trieste's Grand Canal was an important route for the traders that flocked to the city after it was declared a tax-free port in 1719. One of the major industries that sprang up was the importation and processing of coffee. Triestines drink twice as much coffee as anyone else and Trieste is home to the Illy coffee company that supplies 40% of Italy's coffee.

PAGES 196–197: A lone climber gives a sense of perspective and scale to the beautiful peaks of the Dolomites. These geologically unique mountains are regarded by some as the most beautiful in Europe.

ABOVE: This old church in Udine reflects the influence of Venice which ruled over this old Roman frontier town from 1420 to 1797.

RIGHT: The tower of the church of San Filippo and San Giacomo (SS Filippo e Giacomo) tries to compete with the mountains surrounding Cortina d'Ampezzo in the eastern Dolomites.

ABOVE: Old style Alpine charm of the buildings in the center of Cortina d'Ampezzo. The base for the 1956 Winter Olympics, this ski resort now ranks as one of the world's most fashionable winter places to visit.

RIGHT: The Dolomites are a magnet for hikers, mountaineers, and anyone who loves skiing. The village of Sesto is one of the most popular bases for walkers, with numerous trails through the mountains.

PAGES 202–203: Twilight over the Dolomites near Cortina d'Ampezzo. Sitting in the wide and sunny Ampezzo valley in the north of the Veneto region and only about 30 miles from the Austrian border, Cortina offers a range of ski slopes for everyone from beginner to expert.

LEFT: The wines of Alto Adige reflect the unique cultural make up of the region. Italians think of it as a white wine producing area while Germans think of it as red wine producing area. Its high vineyards are mainly owned by small family run concerns and the area has earned a reputation for high quality wines.

PAGE 206: The craggy peaks of the Dolomites are made up of an ancient limestone mix that causes them to change color throughout the day and to become weirdly luminous at night.

PAGE 207: The subtly pale color of this old Christian church, with its shiny onion dome, contrasts beautifully with the fierce cliffs and peaks behind.

Pages 208–209: The little Tyrolean village of Santa Maddalena, with its lush and gentle fields, seems about to be overwhelmed by the tall wave of angry cliffs of rock that form the Odle Massif of the Dolomites.

PERUGIA AND UMBRIA

PERUGIA AND UMBRIA

Situated halfway between Rome and Florence, land-locked Umbria is called the green heart of Italy. The landscape is just as beautiful as neighboring Tuscany, although a little more wild and uncultivated, and it is a mountainous and hilly region with the Apennines forming a high ridge in the east. Evergreen holm oak trees are abundant throughout—thus its epithet—"Green" Umbria. Autumn mists and silvery summer hazes give the local scenery a distinctive, gentle, and otherworldly feel. The forests are full of wild boar and porcupines and Umbria is the only other Italian region, besides Piedmont, where truffles are found, especially around the gastronomic hub of Norcia, justifiably famous for its pork and cheese products. The original inhabitants, around the sixth century B.C., were the "Umbri," thought by the Romans to be the original tribe of Italy. The Etruscans' arrival caused them to disappear into the mountainous east of the region leaving the Etruscans to civilize Umbria and to build many of the important cities before being overrun by the Romans and their mighty empire.

Perugia is the regional capital of Umbria and in common with other Umbrian hilltop towns and cities was built on Etruscan and Roman foundations. An almost perfect example of a classic "city state," Perugia is a university town—many foreign students come here to learn Italian—with long, wide, traffic-free piazzas and annual jazz and chocolate festivals. East of Perugia is Assisi—the most famous city in Umbria. The birthplace, in 1181, of St Francis, Assisi attracts hundreds of thousands of pilgrims to the Basilica di San Francesco, one of Italy's most holy places. The giant Basilica, which holds the saint's body in its crypt, was damaged in the 1997 earthquake that caused widespread damage across much of Umbria. Repairs and restorations are now complete and the Basilica has been

returned to its original thirteenth-century magnificence, apart from one fresco that was too badly damaged to repair completely.

The medieval towns and cities of Umbria are much less overrun by tourists than their equivalents in Tuscany and this tranquility is one of Umbria's many charms, particularly in summer when the crowds can be oppressive. Gubbio, to the north of Perugia, is a perfect Umbrian gem that is delightful to stroll around. Built into the side of Monte Ingino, it has fiercely steep streets, a fourteenth century parliament building called Palazzo dei Consoli, charming shops and restaurants, and never seems over-crowded.

Todi, to the south of Perugia, has been nicknamed "Todiwood" by locals because of the number of Americans who visit and who have bought properties in the countryside nearby. Sitting on a hill overlooking the river Tiber, Todi's Etruscan, Roman, and medieval walls still stand to protect and surround its magnificent Piazza del Popolo.

Orvieto, in the northwestern corner of Umbria, sits, on a plug of volcanic rock that rises 1,000 feet above the valley of the river Paglia. With its sheer sides, the rock was easily defendable, and the city became one of the Etruscan League of 12 Cities. The Romans sacked the city toward the end of the third century B.C., driving the Etruscans west. One of the legacies of the Etruscans is the warren of tunnels, caves, and wells—still usable today—that were dug out of the soft tufo rock under the city. Orvieto prospered under Rome and became a popular country retreat for many popes. In 1290 work began on the city's stupendous gothic cathedral. Commissioned to celebrate the miracle of Bolsena, when blood is said to have emerged from the Holy Eucharist, Orvieto's Duomo has a jaw-dropping facade of elaborate mosaics and marble sculptures that took hundreds of architects, sculptors, painters, and mosaicists more than 300 years to complete.

PAGES 210–211: Ferentillo, between Spoleto and Terni in the valley of Valnerina, is a typical small Umbrian hill town. A ruined castle sits atop a craggy rock surrounded by the houses that would once have been occupied by peasants in service to the local landowner.

BELOW: Castelluccio, one of Italy's highest towns at 4,800 feet, rises gently from the flat and windy Piano Grande beneath the peaks of the Sibillini mountain range.

PAGES 214–215: Assisi is dominated by the Basilica di San Francesco (see pages 218–219) but Assisi's Duomo—as shown here—is San Rufino with its handsome Romanesque design. St. Francis was baptized in this cathedral, as was St. Clare.

LEFT: The rose window on the front of San Rufino in Assisi. The cathedral was built in 1140 to host the body of the martyred Bishop San Rufino. It was he who, in the third century A.D., first preached the Gospel in Assisi before meeting an untimely end in the River Chiascio.

ABOVE: The cloisters of the Abbey of Sassovivo, near Foligno, date from 1229 and are the abbey's finest feature. Originally built by Benedictines on solid rock, the abbey shares its name with the famous Sassovivo water from a nearby spring that is noted for its health benefits.

PAGES 218–219: Basilica of San Francesco, Assisi.

RIGHT: Medieval bridge and aqueduct, Ponte delle Torri, Spoleto, Umbria.

ABOVE: A beautiful doorway leads out to an old cobbled street in the old Roman city of Narni in southern Umbria. Narni is full of Roman remains and in recent times has been linked to C.S Lewis's *Chronicles of Narnia*. Unfortunately for devotees of *The Lion, The Witch and The Wardrobe*, any similarity between Narni and Narnia is just a coincidence.

PAGES 222–223: Mount Subasio, in the background, towers over the plain below Assisi and the quaint town of Spello. The mountain is a national park and lies just west of the Umbrian border with Le Marche.

ABOVE: These windows and arches in Perugia show how well preserved the buildings are in this old city state. The original city remains tranquil with wide streets and wonderful museums. Below the town is a less wonderful area of modern suburbs.

RIGHT: Ponte del Torri aqueduct—San Pietro behind.

224

AVGVSTA PERVSIA MCCCCLXI

LEFT: Umbria's hill towns are full of atmospheric little alleys traversed by highly individual arches that help to support the walls of the buildings on each side.

ABOVE: The semicircular frontispiece to the Oratory of San Bernardino is considered to be the most important Renaissance monument in Perugia. Completed in 1461, it depicts the miracles performed by the saint.

227

DOMBVI
AN
SAL
1059

OPVS
COBI
PIERVTII
49

LEFT: The facade of the Duomo in Orvieto is one of the architectural wonders of Italy, and attracts huge numbers of admirers each year. Some 90 mosaicists worked on the facade over the 300 years it took to complete the work.

ABOVE: Citta di Castello sits on a site by the Tiber first settled by the Romans. Its elegant round bell tower was built in the thirteenth century and the town's medieval and Renaissance center is enclosed by the original sixteenth century walls.

ABOVE: This twelfth century facade of the Duomo in Spoleto has an intricate mosaic facade surrounded by eight rose windows and contains a fresco by Pinturicchio, painted when he was seventeen.

RIGHT: The interior of the Duomo in Spoleto. Built to replace a church destroyed in 1155 by Frederick Barbarossa, the walls are adorned by an icon of the Madonna offered to the city in 1185 by Barbarossa as an apology.

PAGE 232: The Sibillini Mountains of the Apennines dwarf the isolated town of Castellucio as it sits high above the plain of the Piano Grande on the Umbria–Le Marche border.

PAGE 233: Gualdo Tadino's houses have most of their window shutters firmly closed to keep their interiors cool against the heat of the sun. This little town in the far northeast of Umbria is an important center for ceramics.

ABOVE: The Rose Window of Orvieto's Duomo. This spectacular cathedral was commissioned in 1290 by Pope Nicholas IV to celebrate a miracle that occurred 27 years earlier at Bolsena when a priest celebrating mass raised the communion host and blood fell on the altar cloth. With striking black and white walls and an intricately decorated facade, it is a hybrid of Romanesque, Gothic, and Renaissance styles and is regarded as one of the great treasures of Italy.

RIGHT: The Temple of Santa Maria della Consolazione sits in its own little park, overlooking the Tiber, on the outskirts of the picturesque hill town of Todi. The church took 99 years to construct and was completed in 1607. For many, this is the finest Renaissance church in Italy.

LE MARCHE, THE ADRIATIC COAST, AND THE APENNINES

LE MARCHE, THE ADRIATIC COAST, AND THE APENNINES

Sandwiched between the Apennines and the Adriatic Sea, Le Marche is one of the emerging tourist areas of Italy and foreigners are rushing to buy old stone properties here as holiday homes. Many people are just discovering for the first time the region's spectacular mountain scenery, its isolated but beautiful cities such as Urbino and Ascoli Piceno, and its pretty hills rolling down to the coast.

Le Marche's mountains are strongly reminiscent of a little Switzerland. Lush and green in the spring and summer, they become dramatically snowcapped in winter. The region is home to several impressive national parks including Monti Sibillini and Gran Sasso in the south. The Frasassi caves, which date back thousands of years, are one of the region's wonders with giant stalactites, stalagmites and underground lakes.

With a 110-mile coastline, this region has two types of beach resort. San Benedetto del Tronto, Pesaro and Gabicce all have wide sandy beaches on which thousands of sunbeds are laid out during the summer season. It's a noisy, fun atmosphere but those seeking peace may well want to head for smaller resorts such as Portonova, Sirola and Numana, which still have spectacular beaches but also have quieter coves framed by impressive cliffs.

Urbino, in the north, is one of the treasures of Italy. A Renaissance city that in terms of importance was a close competitor to Florence, Urbino hasn't changed much since the fifteenth century. Recognized by UNESCO as a World Heritage Site, Urbino was once a magnet for Renaissance scholars and artists whose work and influence had a profound effect, not only on the city itself, but on the rest of Europe as well.

The city's UNESCO citation reads: "Urbino represents a pinnacle of Renaissance art and architecture, harmoniously adapted to its physical site and to its medieval precursor in an exceptional manner." The city fell into economic stagnation from the sixteenth century and this decline actually preserved the glorious architecture of domes and towers, which might have been demolished otherwise. The enormous Palazzo Ducale dominates the city and is regarded as a peerless example of Renaissance values. Within its walls is the

National Museum with an outstanding collection of art. Experts consider the museum's treasures to be one of the best Renaissance collections in the world.

In the far south of Marche is the other classic town of the region, Ascoli Piceno. A charming valley town, Ascoli Piceno has, at its heart, the beautiful Piazza del Popolo, a magnificent square surrounded by medieval buildings including the thirteenth century Palazzo del Popolo. Ancient watchtowers look down over the river Tronto as it runs through Ascoli. This old town can easily be seen in a day but, as they say, "never forgotten."

PAGES 236–237: One figure reads and another, on the Duomo of Urbino, gazes out over the perfectly preserved city below. The Duomo is attached to the immense Palazzo Ducale and the building's architecture reflects the Renaissance philosophy of nobility and purity.

PAGE 238: Ravenna is famed for its mosaics. The city was once, briefly, the capital of the Roman Empire but in the sixth century was overrun by Byzantines whose eastern influence is still visible today in the mosaics that decorate many of the town's most important buildings. It is on the Adriatic coast of Emilia Romagna.

THIS PICTURE: The fortress prisons of Mount Titano, in the tiny independent state of San Marino to the north of Le Marche. Rocca Guaita (center) the largest of three prisons on the mountain's peaks was built in the tenth century and functioned until the 1960s. Rocca Cesta, to its right, dates from the thirteenth century and is now a museum.

LEFT: Urbino's first World Heritage Site citation says: "During its short cultural pre-eminence, Urbino attracted some of the most outstanding humanist scholars and artists of the Renaissance, who created there an exceptional urban complex of remarkable homogeneity, the influence of which carried far into the rest of Europe."

ABOVE: The Palazzo Ducale literally climbs all over the steep isolated hill that Urbino sits on. Today it is a flourishing university town that attracts students from all over the world.

PAGES 242–243: Urbino's second World Heritage Site citation says: "Urbino represents a pinnacle of Renaissance art and architecture, harmoniously adapted to its physical site and to its medieval precursor in an exceptional manner."

LEFT: Lions guard the Gothic entrance to Ancona's eleventh-century Duomo San Ciriaco. The church survived the aerial bombing that devastated most of this port city during World War II.

ABOVE AND RIGHT: Ravenna's Duomo Sant'Orso was built in the eighteenth century on top of a church founded by St. Ursus in 396 A.D. The fifth century Baptistery, next to the Duomo, contains the oldest mosaic in Ravenna showing the baptism of Christ. The round Campanile behind the Duomo is tenth century and was part of the site's original church.

PAGES 246–247: Le Marche is an impressive mountainous and hilly region. With Ancona now on European flight schedules, this area is very popular for British and German families wishing to purchase an Italian property.

STVDIORVM · VNIVERSITATI · FASTIGIVM

LEFT AND PAGE 250: On the north side of the Piazza Duca Federico sits Urbino cathedral. In 1789 the earlier cathedral was almost completely destroyed by an earthquake, the replacement building was rebuilt and redesigned in 1801 in neo-Paladian style by Giuseppe Valadier, who also added a cupola.

ABOVE: The enormous Palazzo Ducale, built by the great artistic patron Duke Federico da Montefeltro in the fifteenth century, dominates Urbino and now houses the National Museum of Le Marche with one of the best collections of Renaissance art anywhere in the world.

PAGE 251: The campanile or bell tower of the church of San Francesco in Urbino. Originally dating from the thirteenth century, it houses the tombs of Antonio and Oddantonio da Montefeltro who were the parents of the great artist Raphael.

253

Only 15,000 people live in Urbino, but its size is not representative of its artistic significance—it is one of Italy's most important Renaissance cities. The Duomo was completed in 1789 but badly damaged in the 1997 earthquake. It is now fully restored.

The Apennines mountain range can be seen in the background of this photograph of countryside near Urbino. The central and southern Apennines have mineral springs, crater lakes, fumaroles, and volcanoes (two, Vesuvius and Etna, are still very much on the active list).

RIGHT: The abundant grassy hillsides of western Le Marche were once home to the ancient Picenians. Great traders of their time, the Picenians prospered through their proximity to the Adriatic and traded with Greeks and Phoenicians.

PAGES 258–259: South of Le Marche in Abruzzo at nearly 4,800 feet above sea level stands the unique Rocca di Calascio. A solitary 33-foot tower was built in the thirteenth century on the edge of the plateau and later, in the fifteenth century, higher walls and four buttressing round towers were built around it. Designed to accommodate troops, the castle is not as big as those that acted as refuges for local populations.

It is known as "The Big Rock of Italy" and Gran Sasso, and its National Park, attracts walkers and climbers who enjoy the wide open space of the great high plain of Campo Imperatore and the 9,300-foot "big rock" itself.

Lake Campotosto is man-made, Europe's largest artificial lake, and an important nature reserve.

TURIN AND PIEDMONT

TURIN AND PIEDMONT

Piedmont means "foot of the mountains" and refers to the fact that this region of Italy sits at the foot of the Alps. It is bordered by France to the west, Switzerland and Valle D'Aosta to the north, Lombardy and Emilia-Romagna to the east, and Liguria to the south. The region is noted for its historic castles set in beautiful mountain scenery and is one of the most important wine-growing areas of Italy—producing classic red wines such as Barolo and Barbaresco. Piedmont also produces the perennially popular Martini and Cinzano vermouths.

Turin is the capital of Piedmont and this big, sprawling industrial city is the heart of Italy's car manufacturing business —the Fiat automobile company was established here in 1899 and after having undergone some lean years is now flourishing again. Turin is also a beautiful Baroque city with distinct French influences, grand boulevards, and striking architecture. There is a sophisticated cafe culture and locals and visitors alike enjoy wonderfully elegant coffee shops and bars that are perfect for a morning cappuccino, a pre-dinner aperitivo, or an after-dinner digestivo.

The Italian Royals held court in this region until their abdication and ultimate exile in 1946 and the Savoy Royal Palace is one of Turin's most popular destinations, along with the Holy Shroud—Sindone—which resides in the custom-built Cappella della Sindone at the back of Turin's Duomo. This four-yard sheet of linen is thought by millions

of people around the world to be the burial shroud of Jesus Christ and to bear the imprint of his crucified body. It was brought to Turin by Duke Emanuele Filiberto in 1578 and remains a hugely controversial religious relic. Using carbon dating, at least three scientific studies have said that it is a forgery, probably created by some well-meaning artist in the late thirteenth or fourteenth century.

Nevertheless the shroud remains an important part of the history of Turin and is displayed in public on rare and very special occasions. A convincing replica of the Sindone is on permanent display for visitors.

Leaving Turin, the countryside around Alba and Asti is famous for white truffles, which can sell for as much as $2,000 per pound. Alba has the largest dedicated white truffle market anywhere in the world and is at its busiest in October and November. The heavenly aroma released when a truffle is shaved over pasta is one of the great olfactory delights of Italy,

In the north of the region lies Lake Maggiore, Italy's second largest, and the tiny but perfectly formed Lake Orta. Both are popular water sports centers and idyllic places to spend the long, hot summers.

In the far west lies the Valle Di Susa, recently home to the 2006 Winter Olympics. While some ski resorts such as Sestriere are modern and over-developed, they nevertheless have fabulous ski trails, some of which lead into France, and the challenging skiing attracts sports enthusiasts from all over the world.

The mighty river Po, Italy's longest, also has its source here beneath the peak of Monte Viso, on the border with France. It flows eastward for 405 miles through Turin and across Lombardy, just south of Milan before entering the Adriatic near Venice.

PAGES 264–265: The introduction to the Italian constitution states that "Italy is a nation founded and based on work" and Turin, the busy capital of Piemonte—Piedmont—is the very embodiment of these words. With an elegant, French-influenced, city center of wide boulevards and pretty arcades full of fine cafés there is a lively cultural atmosphere to be savored.

LEFT: Aosta Duomo is a mix of the fifth, sixth, and fifteenth centuries. The twin bell towers are from the tenth-century cathedral and inside is a precious A.D. 406 ivory carving depicting the Roman Emperor Honorius. The city is still surrounded by its original Roman walls, with pride of place going to a 25 B.C. arch celebrating the capture of the city from the Celts.

LEFT: The spire of La Mole Antonelliana immeditely identifies this as the city of Turin in Torino Province. It was designed by the architect Alessandro Antonelli and built between 1863 and 1889 and is now part of the National Museum of Cinema.

RIGHT: Turin at night..

BELOW RIGHT: Verres, in the south of the Valle d'Aosta, is a popular destination for mountaineers and sightseers to the lower Alps. The Mount Avic Regional Park contains many ibex, a species of wild mountain goat.

LEFT: Val d'Aosta is an easy drive from Turin and the peak of Monte Bianco (Mont Blanc) is accessible by cable car from the Italian side. The viewing platform, at 11,000 feet, gives panoramic views across the Italian and French Alps. Chamonix, on the French side, is served by a cable car so lunch in France is an easy option.

ABOVE LEFT: The massive Gran Paradiso National Park was once owned by King Vittorio Emanuele II, Italy's first king after Unification in 1870, and was bequeathed to the nation after World War 1.

LEFT: Castle Serre in Val d'Aosta.

ABOVE: The little chapel of Gressoney-St-Jean is idyllically set in the Val d'Aosta. This is the least populated and smallest region in Italy but the numbers are inflated by its status as a popular holiday area for both winter and summer vacations.

PAGES 274–275: Visitors to the glorious Gran Paradiso National Park wilderness can stay overnight in the Park's mountain refuges and watch as nature puts on a spellbinding display at sunset.

PAGE 276

ABOVE: Another view of Gran Paradiso National Park at sunset.

BELOW: Built in the midfourteenth century by a member of the Savoy family, Castello Fenis lives up to everyone's fantasy of what a castle should look like, with turrets, towers and battlements and even portcullises. Visitors can see the impressive collection of weapons in the armory as well the medieval kitchens, complete with original utensils and pots and pans.

PAGE 277: The glaciers in the Alps are the source of many of Europe's biggest rivers and their spring melt can cause flooding as far away as Bulgaria and Romania.

RIGHT: The vineyards of Valle d'Aosta are the highest in Italy. Often sited above 3,000 feet, the vines flourish despite being planted in rocky soil.

GENOA AND THE ITALIAN RIVIERA

GENOA AND THE ITALIAN RIVIERA

With its mild winters and sheltered coast, Liguria is often described as the Riviera dei Fiori (Riviera of Flowers) because of its microclimate, which allows plants and flowers to be grown commercially all year round. This may be one of the smallest of the Italian regions, but to many Liguria conjures up the perfect image of Italy by the sea. Picturesque fishing villages, little towns clinging to steep cliffs, and the startlingly blue Ligurian Sea are well loved by visitors. The Italian Riviera itself is 218 miles in length and stretches from the French border to the west to Tuscany in the south.

Genoa, the region's capital and Italy's busiest seaport, sits in the middle of the Ligurian coast and most visitors to the Italian Riviera simply head for the beach and ignore this ancient center of maritime power and trade. Genoa, once known as La Superba (The Proud), had an empire that stretched from North Africa to Syria and the Black Sea. A

gateway for the spice trade, adventurers, and the armies of the Crusades, Genoa claims Christopher Columbus as its most famous son and his childhood home is open to the public. The city also has one of the largest medieval quarters in Europe and the legacy of this great port's former glory can still be seen in the thirteen magnificent patrician palaces, built within ten years starting in 1554, on either side of the herring-boned pavement of Via Garibaldi. Genoa has magnificent churches and some of the best food in Italy. Genovese salami and pesto are famous worldwide and Ligurians claim that true pesto can only be made with their local smooth, small-leafed basil and olive oil from groves clinging to the steeply stepped hillsides above the Italian Riviera coast.

The Italian Riviera is, in fact, made up of two distinct sections on either side of Genoa. The Riviera di Ponente (Riviera of the Setting Sun) runs from Ventimiglia, on the

French border, to Genoa in the east. San Remo, its most famous resort, was once a major stopover on "the Grand Tour," the social enrichment journey for lucky, young, rich Britons. Popular with royalty, the wealthy, and artists (Tchaikovsky and the Russian Royal family were regular visitors because they wanted to escape the harsh Russian winters), San Remo's glory days were the last thirty years of the nineteenth century and up to the beginning of World War II. Boasting some of the world's finest hotels, a beautiful promenade, and a casino, San Remo was as glamorous as its French neighbors Cannes and Nice. Today it remains a popular vacation spot and is famous worldwide for its annual music festival and for its flower market, which sells the wares of 6,500 growers, and exports cut flowers and ornamental greenery all over the world.

From Genoa to La Spezia is the Riviera di Levante (Riviera of the Rising Sun) with quieter and more beautiful beaches and the internationally renowned resorts of Portofino and Rapallo, where the jet set comes out to play in vast yachts. Portofino, first made famous by vacationing Hollywood couples including Humphrey Bogart and Lauren Bacall, and Richard Burton and Elizabeth Taylor,

remains a playground of the rich and famous and is one of the most expensive property hotspots in the country. Farther down the coast is the Cinque Terre (Five Lands) peninsula with its spectacular landscape and dazzling views. The five little fishing villages of Vernazza, Monterosso al Mare, Corniglia, Manarola, and Riomaggiore all hang precariously from the rocky terrain and until relatively recently the only way to travel between them was on foot.

PAGE 280–281: The Church of San Giacomo, Santa Margherita Ligure, on the beautiful Portofino peninsula.

BELOW LEFT: Camogli is a pretty harbor community established on the edge of a promontory and nature reserve known as the Portofino Peninsula. This small village is protected by a massive seventeenth-century sea wall.

BELOW: The candy-colored houses of La Spezia are piled higgledy-piggledy on top of each other in this large port town, one of the liveliest of the Riviera communities. Although it has an industrial hub, La Spezia also has palm-lined promenades and parks filled with orange and lemon trees.

ABOVE: San Bartolomeo al Mare is another jewel of the Italian Riviera right next to Cervo. The thirteenth-century bell tower is all that remains of the original medieval church that was destroyed by an earthquake in 1887.

RIGHT: A former Roman colony, Portofino has also been ruled by the French, the Spanish, the Austrians, and the English and is now a picture perfect harbor town overlooking the turquoise Ligurian Sea. This little resort has some of the most expensive real estate in Italy.

LEFT: Genoa's Palazzo Ducale—ducal palace—was built in the twelfth century. It became the seat of the first Genoese Doge, Simon Boccanegrathe, in 1339. The central part of the palace was destroyed by fire in 1777 and reconstructed in neoclassical style.

ABOVE: Rapallo was sacked by pirates in 1549 and its castle was built in 1551 to defend the town from future raids. The walls are seven-foot thick and the lower windows were originally openings for cannons giving defenders of the building a full 360 degrees' field of fire.

ABOVE: With its brightly colored houses built in haphazard fashion, the little town of Manorola is also the center of the Cinque Terre winemaking area.

ABOVE RIGHT: The lighthouse of Punta del Capo on the Portofino promontory has been a beacon of safety over the years and remains a famous landmark. It is now possible to walk over the rock to the lighthouse and enjoy spectacular views of the Gulf of Tigullio.

RIGHT: The Cinque Terre are five villages clinging to a wild rocky outcrop on the Riviera di Levante. Despite their relative inaccessibility they are hugely popular destinations for tourists.

ABOVE: Genoa has always been associated with the sea both as a port and as a birthplace of sailors— Christopher Columbus was born here. This view looks out over the port.

RIGHT: Genoa's Chiesa del Gesu, next to the Palazzo Ducale in the medieval quarter of the city, has a fine interior of colored marble floors and frescoes. The highlights are two magnificent works by master artist Rubens: *Circoncisione* and *S. Ignazio Guarisce un'Ossessa.*

ABOVE: Genoa's Old Town.

RIGHT: With its many pretty harbors full of tiny fishing craft the Cinque Terre region is a piscatorial paradise and many of Liguria's culinary specialties are based around the fruits of the sea. One of the most popular is *cacciucco*, a rich and filling fish soup.

LEFT: The Palazzo San Giorgio in Genoa was constructed in 1260 as the first major palace of the city. Enlarged in 1570 with frescoes painted by Lorenzo Tavarone, the building can be toured by the public on appointment only.

ABOVE: The romantic gardens of the Villa Durazzo-Pallavicini were designed and laid out between 1840 and 1846. Its temples and artificial lakes were built for the Marchesa Clelia Durazzo by her nephew Ignazio Pallavicini.

PAGES 296–297: Sitting in restaurants and cafés, watching fishing boats sail in and out of the little harbors, is one of the most pleasant ways to spend a day in this part of Italy.

LEFT: Vineyards cloak the hills that sweep down from the charming Ligurian hill town of La Morra. Famous for its white wines—such as vermentino and pigato—and its reds—dolceacqua and rossese—the town has its own wine museum and guided walks around the vineyards.

NAPLES AND THE AMALFI COAST

NAPLES AND THE AMALFI COAST

The region of Campania is home to the city of Naples and one of the finest and most famous coastlines in Italy—the beautiful Amalfi coast, better known as the Neapolitan Riviera. Because of its natural beauty and extraordinary architectural ruins—Pompeii, Herculaneum, Paestum, and the Phlegrean Fields to name a few—this is one of the most visited regions of Italy. The active volcano Vesuvius dominates the area and sits 4,200 feet above the coastline, just to the south of Naples, in broody magnificence. It is considered one of the world's most dangerous volcanoes, because up to 3 million people live and work in the surrounding area.

Vesuvius' deadly eruption of A.D. 79 deposited 10 feet of rocks and ash on Pompeii and tourists flock to see the excavations that have revealed the skeleton of a working Roman city frozen in time—complete streets with homes, theaters, shops, kitchens, bakeries, and an almost perfectly preserved Roman amphitheater. The anfiteatro once seated 20,000 spectators and is the oldest surviving amphitheater in Italy. Herculaneum, to the west of Pompeii, was drowned by a giant wave of boiling mud after Pompeii's burial by ash. This elegant coastal resort was a Roman version of Long Island's Hamptons. It was a place where the Roman elite could escape and pass lazy days in elegant villas cooled by sea breezes. The mud entered every crack and corner of every building and as a result Herculaneum is better preserved than Pompeii, though so far only half has been excavated.

Naples, the birthplace of pizza and Sophia Loren, has been described by Herbert Kubly in his book American in

PAGES 300–301: San Francesco di Paola in Naples was constructed as an imitation of the Pantheon in Rome. Begun in 1817 and completed 29 years later, its dome reaches to a height 173 feet over the Piazza del Plebiscito.

BELOW AND RIGHT: The Temple of Ceres is one of Paestum's remarkably preserved Greek temples that stands on the site of the ancient city of Poseidonia which was founded by the Greeks in the seventh century B.C.

Italy as "an eternally unfolding play." Love it or hate it (and many people do), it is a city that never stands still. Famous for the breathtaking recklessness of its drivers as well as the beauty of its churches, fortresses, royal palaces, arcades, boulevards, and tiny bustling streets with colorful markets, it can be an intimidating place but one well worth getting to know. Its Museo Archeologico Nazionale is one of the finest museums in Europe with a vast collection of Greek and Roman treasures as well as most of the excavated finds from Pompeii and Herculaneum, including wall paintings, mosaics, and everyday household objects. Just north of the city is another must-see landmark, the Royal Palace of Caserta. Completed in 1774 this is Italy's own Versailles, complete with 1,200 rooms of treasures and a beautifully laid out park.

South of Vesuvius, the gulfs of Naples and Salerno are divided by a peninsula and here you will find the well-loved tourist destinations of Sorrento, Positano, Amalfi, Ravello, and Salerno. The playgrounds of the rich and famous as well as countless artists, composers, and writers, the towns are all laid out on a beautiful-but-tortuous 44-mile road. A short trip by ferry from Sorrento takes you to the islands of Capri—still a trendy holiday spot and crammed with wonderful boutiques, hotels, and restaurants—and Ischia, which is famous for its mud baths and spa facilities.

Because of Campania's volcanic soil, the fertile farmland in this part of the country produces truly stupendous fruit and vegetables, bursting with color and flavor. The lemons of the Amalfi coast, in particular, are renowned worldwide, as is as the liqueur that is made from them, Limoncello. There are also herds of water buffalo that produce the creamy buffalo cheese called mozzarella, which is highly prized by gourmets and distributed all over the world.

BELOW: One of the most beautiful and most visited coastlines in Italy, the Amalfi Coast has breathtaking views wherever you look.

RIGHT: The roads of the Amalfi coast from Sorrento to Salerno are not for faint-hearted drivers because of the hairpin bends that run perilously close to the high cliff edges. But they do offer incredible views.

PAGES 306–307: The Greek temples of Paestum include the magnificent Temple of Poseidon, the best-preserved Doric temple anywhere in the world.

LEFT: In A.D. 79, the cities of Herculaneum and Pompeii were buried under deep layers of ash after the volcano Vesuvius erupted. The towns were lost to the world for some 1,600 years before they were rediscovered with many of their buildings and contents still intact, giving us a unique insight into the life of Romans in the first century.

BELOW: Blue skies dotted with powder-puff clouds and a breathtaking view of the Bay of Naples from this balcony typifies the scenic charms of the region of Campania.

BELOW: Towering 4,200 feet above the coastline, the active volcano Vesuvius looms over Naples. Considered one of the most dangerous volcanoes in the world, city authorities have evacuation plans in hand should it decide to unleash its awesome power in the future.

RIGHT: Properties overlooking the Amalfi Coast often have a series of stepped terraces or balconies with heart stopping views over the Gulf of Naples and the Gulf of Salerno.

ABOVE: The tiny fishing town of Atrani was founded as a seaside retreat for the Roman aristocracy and has continued to be the haunt of some of the most powerful Amalfi families.

RIGHT: The little ports and the calm harbors of the Amalfi are to be found tucked away beneath sheer cliffs. The Amalfi Peninsula divides the Gulf of Naples from the Gulf of Salerno to the south.

PAGES 314–315: "See Naples and Die" is an expression that has been in use for over 2,000 years. Meaning different things to different people—Virgil used it referring to the city's beauty —there is no doubt that Naples, one of the most vibrant and exciting cities, divides people into those who love it and those who hate it.

PAGES 316–317: Positana tumbles down the Amalfi Coast
to the Mediterranean Sea.

LEFT: The Fontana dell'Immacolatella on the Naples
seafront was built in 1601 by Michelangelo Naccherino
and Pietro Bernini, the father of the great fountain
designer and sculptor Gian Lorenzo Bernini.

THIS PICTURE: John Steinbeck described living in Positano
on the Amalfi Coast this way: "You do not walk to visit a
friend, you either climb or slide."

BARI AND THE SOUTH

The heel, arch, and toe of Italy's "boot" are made up of the regions of Puglia, Basilicata, and Calabria. The last two are known in Italy as the mezzogiorno —the literal translation is midday—because of the fierceness of the sun that burns down on them.

Puglia has a long coastline facing the Ionian and Adriatic seas and is a region full of historic towns, Roman and Greek ruins, and seaside resorts such as Otranto and Gallipoli. It also produces more olive oil and wine than anywhere else in Italy and is famous for its strange beehive-shaped dwellings called trulli, which are mainly sited around the town of Alberobello.

The jewel of Puglia is the university town of Lecce, which has been described as a "Florence of the south" with its ornate architecture and vibrant restaurants, bars, and shops. Crammed with buildings crafted from the local rose-tinted sandstone and covered by intricately carved designs of angels, cherubs, devils, monsters, fruit, and flowers, it's a delightful base from which to explore the region.

Bari, the capital of Puglia, has a maze-like old quarter with tiny, narrow streets—Vecchia Bari—as well as broad boulevards. Bari was once the great gateway to and from the east and was the point of arrival for the Phoenicians who came with their own vines and thus introduced Italians to the art of making wine. Situated on the end of the great Via Appia, it was also the departure point for Romans traveling to their empire in the east.

Puglia's eastern neighboring region Basilicata boasts the highest regional capital in Italy—Potenza—which stands at more than 2,500 foot above sea level. Basilicata can seem a

forbidding place to many people—it is one of the poorest Italian regions and 90 percent of it is covered by mountains or hills—but it possesses a hauntingly beautiful sense of desolation in its arid, scorched landscape. Basilicata also has some of Italy's best beaches with crystal clear waters and fine, golden sand.

Matera, in the eastern part of the region, was declared a World Heritage site by UNESCO in 1993. Home to "the most outstanding, intact example of a troglodyte settlement in the Mediterranean region," this town of cave dwellings carved out of rock was used by Mel Gibson in *The Passion of the Christ* because of its similarity to Jerusalem and its environs. "The first time I saw it, I just went crazy, because it was so perfect," Gibson said about Matera. Ever-resourceful Materans now conduct guided tours based on the film and tourists can even sleep in the hotel room occupied by the film star during shooting.

The toe of Italy's boot is formed by Calabria, a wild and very underdeveloped region with a largely inaccessible mountainous interior. With a history of being overrun by outsiders, Calabria has been ruled and influenced by Greeks (the great mathematician Pythagoras lived in Crotone, a center of science and learning in the sixth century B.C.), Romans, Northern Goths, and Arabs, along with conquerors from Lombardy, Saracens, and Normans—to name just a few. In quick succession the French, Spanish, Neapolitans, and Austrians also had their turn at ruling over Calabria.

This constant invasion by outsiders has left the Calabrese fiercely self sufficient, but they are warm and hospitable people and with its wonderful coastline with pristine beaches, Calabria is not to be underestimated in terms of charm and natural beauty. The interior is made up of the densely forested Calabrese Appenines, snow clad in winter, where the local people create beautiful wood-carvings and blankets. Lemons, almonds, date palms, figs, bergamot (as used in Earl Grey Tea), and bananas are grown in Calabria.

PAGES 320–321: These odd cone-shaped buildings called "trulli" are only found in Puglia. Trulli have prehistoric origins and are made from limestone rocks gathered from the surrounding area and then, without mortar, laid on top of each other to form the walls of these distinctive little houses.

LEFT: Alberobello's church tower among the stone roofs belonging to the trulli, for which it is famous.

PAGES 324–325: The Cathedral in Trani, on the northern Puglia coast, was completed in 1143 and boasts fine bronze doors surrounded by an Arab-influenced Romanesque portal. The doors were hung in 1175 and the Duomo sits in its own large square facing the sea. The clean sun-bleached limestone of the exterior of Trani Cathedral features beautiful Romanesque style carvings and pillars. Over 100 years in the making, it is regarded as one of the most beautiful buildings in Puglia.

LEFT: The magnificent front of Lecce's baroque Santa Croce Church—to be found in the Piazza della Prefettura. The church's facade was begun in 1548 and completed from 1697 onward. Adjoining it on the north is the extensive and richly ornamented facade of the Celestine convent which belonged to the church; now Palazzo del Governo.

PAGES 328–329: The bones of Saint Nicholas, patron saint of sailors and children, are buried beneath the altar of the Basilica di San Nicola in Bari, Puglia. The cathedral was built in the eleventh century as a home for the relics of the saint and lies at the center of Bari's medieval quarter.

LEFT: Emperor Frederick II built the octagonal Castel del Monte, near Melfi in Puglia, in the thirteenth century. Its unique mathematical configuration—eight octagonal towers surround an octagonal courtyard—has earned it a World Heritage Site listing and has bemused experts of medieval military architecture for centuries.

ABOVE LEFT: The Riviera Calabrese stretches from Amantea to Tropea on the Gulf of Saint Eufemia. Rocky stretches, with occasional towns and villages hanging over the edge, are broken up by sandy beaches with some of the clearest seas to be found around the Italian coast.

ABOVE: This fearsome lion, on the side of Barletta Cathedral, reflects the mix of Romanesque and Gothic styles that were used in its twelfth-century construction. Its exterior and pillars are adorned by a variety of mermaids and monsters.

LEFT: The fifteenth century Duomo of Ostuni is made from local stone and features a rose window with twenty-four rays. Ostuni, to the south of Bari, is known as the "Citta Bianca"—White City —and is a typical Apulian small town, filled with narrow streets and brilliant white buildings.

BELOW: The 400 trulli of Alberobello have been designated a World Heritage Site by UNESCO. This little town is made up of four hills, all covered by trulli whose shape and size gives the visitor the impression of having entered an ancient and miniaturized theme park

LEFT: Svevo Castle was built in 1136 by Ruggero the Norman who was the principal architect of Bari's civil and economic expansion after a long period of Byzantine rule. Destroyed by a subsequent Byzantine attack on the city the castle was rebuilt and modernized by Frederick II in the thirteenth century and was further remodelled in the sixteenth century by Isabella, Duchess of Bari. It is now a museum and home to the Puglia Department of Culture.

PAGE 336: The single-story trulli are a triumph of the art of dry-stone walling and this singular form of building had another purpose as well. During the Middle Ages new buildings accrued high taxes and legend has it that the trulli were an elegant way of avoiding the taxman. Warned of a visit, the trullo owner would simply pull down the stones until the inspector had left whereupon it was rebuilt in a relatively short time.

PAGE 337: Thanks to their peculiar construction these wonderful little houses stay cool in the fierce Puglian summers and are easy to heat during winter. They are now keenly sought after by outsiders wishing to purchase property in Puglia.

LEFT: The coastal waters of Puglia, Basilicata, and Calabria are some of the most inviting. Some of the best beaches are to be found in the Gulf of Taranto, under the arch of Italy's boot, which has warm clear waters and plentiful sea life.

BELOW: The church of Santa Maria Dell'Isola was an ancient Benedictine cathedral off Tropea, a picturesque Calabrian town.

PAGES 340–341: The Pugliese call their olive oil "Green Gold." Puglia is Italy's biggest producer of olive oil and with over 50 million trees has a history of olive cultivation that goes back to 5000 B.C.

LEFT: Ostuni, on a little hill inland between Bari and Brindisi, is a gem of a city with Baroque touches, such as this doorway, due to its being ruled by successive Spanish and French conquerors. It was not until the 1860s that an Italian flag finally flew over this dazzlingly whitewashed city with its tiny streets and classic Mediterranean architecture.

RIGHT: Locorotondo sits on a high ridge overlooking the Itria Valley and its trulli, vineyards, and olive groves. Besides being in the *Guinness Book of Records* as the only city in the world with five "o's" in its name, Locorotondo is full of calm little lanes and is a charming cultural and gastronomic center.

PAGE 344: Italians are quietly competitive and appreciative of the floral window boxes and hanging baskets that decorate the windows of their homes. Cascades of pinks and reds brighten up the view from inside and give tiny alleyways, like this one in Locorotondo, an enchanting atmosphere.

PAGE 345: The little fishing village of Pizzo on the Calabrian coast has become a popular tourist destination for people looking to sample the quieter end of Italian resorts. With sandy beaches, overlooked by a castle dating from 1495, Pizzo's coast is also full of caves and coves that are only accessible from the sea.

LEFT: The church of San Domenico in Cosenza, Calabria, stands above flood walls on the banks of the Busento River that cuts through this old town that pre-dates the Romans. Alaric I, the leader of the Visigoths and conqueror of Rome, is said to have been buried under the river after his early death at 34. Cosenza was also where Isabella of Aragon died, falling from her horse while returning from the Crusades.

BELOW LEFT AND BELOW: The "Mother Church" towers over the dazzlingly white building of Locorotondo. The town was originally named San Giorgio after St. George but an evolutionary series of name changes ended with it being named after its ring-like shape.

PALERMO AND SICILY

PALERMO AND SICILY

The largest island in the Mediterranean, measuring 112 miles from north to south and 170 miles east to west, Sicily has been a magnet for colonization for more than three thousand years. Originally conquered by a southern tribe from the north known as the Siculi, it was subsequently ruled by the Phoenicians, then the Greeks—most importantly in Siracusa in 734 B.C.—and thereafter by the Romans, Arabs, Normans, Spanish, and finally the Italians. All these civilizations have left their cultural footprints on the island in terms of architecture, language, customs, and cuisine, making Sicily one of the most fascinating and cosmopolitan places in Europe.

Visitors are thrilled by the timeless beauty of the scenery. This is a place of rugged hills, ancient olive groves and vineyards, fields planted with lemon, orange, and almond trees, heavenly beaches, and dramatic coastlines. Europe's tallest —and one of the world's most active—volcanoes, Mount Etna, towers over the cities of Catania and Taormina, its sulfurous steam rising from its 10,900-foot summit. The capital city of Palermo is a noisy and chaotic but exciting place where you can soak up the atmosphere of outdoor markets such as the famous fish bazaar Vucceria or sit in a pavement café in the Kalsa quarter with an iced coffee and sweet Sicilian pastries. However, like all cities, it is plagued with traffic problems but there are many gracious and historic piazzas, filled with statues and wonderfully lush and exotic palm trees, where visitors can escape for a few quiet moments.

Sicily also contains some of the best-preserved archaeological sites in Europe such as the Roman amphitheater and Greek temple of Apollo in Siracusa, the Doric Temple of Zeus in Agrigento—a two thousand-year-old olive tree still flourishes in the grounds—and the beautifully preserved fourth-century mosaic pavements in the Roman villa at Casale in the center of the island.

Fiercely hot in the summer months, the island is usually mild and sunny for most of the year but there is an occasional dusting of snow, with correspondingly cold temperatures, in January or February. The best time of the year to travel inland is from April to June, when the countryside is covered with wildflowers, crops are flourishing, and everything is beautifully green.

PAGES 348–349: On Sicily's south coast, near the town of Agrigento, is the Valley of the Temples. One of the island's major tourist attractions, these edifices are remnants of the Greek colony that was founded here in the sixth century B.C.

LEFT: Early morning in Sicily is the best time to see the astonishing assortment of fish on sale in the island's many fish markets, including these splendid specimens on a market stall in Trapani.

ABOVE: Dating from the sixth century B.C., the eight pillars of the Temple of Hercules bear witness to the past splendor of this part of Italy. The large Doric temple originally had 38 columns.

LEFT: Towering 2,450 feet above sea level, the charming medieval town of Erice has two castles. Pepoli castle has foundations dating from Saracen times and Venus castle dates from the era of the Normans and is built on the ruins of the ancient Temple of Venus.

BELOW: The port of Trapani is the departure point for many of the boats to nearby islands such as Pantelleria and is also well-used by local fishing craft whose catches are then flown to mainland Italy and to other parts of the world.

PAGES 354–355: Palermo's massive, rectangular cathedral is known by the name Santa Maria Assunta and is a bizarre but engaging hotch-potch of architectural styles. Some scholars believe a Roman temple once existed here but the building was started in 1072 by the Normans and completed a century later. Over the ages there were Gothic and Baroque renovations and additions.

LEFT: The tricolored flag of Italy flutters in the breeze from the balcony of a patriotic home-owner on the island of Favignana.

ABOVE: Lying off the coast, between the town of Trapani and Marsala, the little island of Favignana is bare and brown during the hot summer months and is named after the Favonio wind that sweeps the territory.

PAGE 358: The Sacrament of First Communion is an important event in the lives of Catholic Italian children, where young people dress in special clothes and are feted by their families who celebrate with a big lunch after the church ceremony.

PAGE 359: Fishing is hard work but it's colorful too. Freshly-painted oars in bright blue dry in the sun on the island of Favignana.

LEFT: Cefalu is a small Sicilian fishing port, squashed onto every available inch of land beneath a huge crag, La Rocca. Surrounded by sandy beaches, it is a haven for sunlovers in summer who flock to this idyllic white-washed town by the sea.

PAGE 362: The provincial capital of southeastern Sicily, Ragusa is renowned for its stunning palazzos and churches which include the Cathedral of San Giorgio, topped by a neoclassical dome and framed by massive ornate columns and a flight of 250 steps leading to the front. An earthquake in 1693 destroyed much of the city but it was rebuilt, with many of the city's Baroque buildings dating from this period.

PAGE 363: Architects who rebuilt Ragusa after the earthquake copied Baroque designs from the cities of Noto and Catania and many fine examples of this type of architecture can be found in this small, quiet town that is said to have one of the highest qualities of life in southern Italy.

PAGES 364–365: Magnificient Mount Etna is Sicily's greatest natural attraction as well as being its highest mountain and Europe's highest active volcano. Some 13,000 square feet of its surface is covered with solidified lava. It is termed a stratovolcano, because of its relatively cool lava temperatures and numerous openings or vents.

LEFT AND ABOVE: The Temples of Castor and Pollux are massive in scale when seen up close but are not as they would have been centuries ago. A reconstruction of the stone columns and posts in 1836 apparently put together different parts of different buildings, rather like making a mistake in a giant jigsaw puzzle.

THIS PICTURE: Strolling along the white sandy beach near Cefalu as night falls and bypassing the brightly colored fishing boats that have been brought ashore is a pleasant excursion before going to dinner in a local trattoria.

RIGHT: A fine example of the beauty of Italy's architecture is displayed in this typical Milazzo façade on via Garibaldi, with a frame of stone carvings and weathered wooden shutters.

The grandeur of Sicily takes the visitor by surprise with its vistas stretching way into the distance. At its best in spring when wild flowers carpet the hillsides, this is one of the best views of the countryside outside the delightful town Piazza Armerina in the center of the island. Set on a plateau about 2,000 feet above sea level, the town is famed for its Roman villa and magnificent displays of mosaics depicting scenes from daily life.

PAGE 372: Like a castle in a fairytale, Pepoli Turret clings to the mountainside and would have been used in the old days to stand guard over the town of Erice.

PAGE 373: The multilayered rooftops of towns in Sicily, using every inch of space, give it a chaotic charm and don't leave much room for inhabitants to have gardens, only terraces from which to catch the setting sun. Television satellite dishes add a modern touch along with lines of freshly laundered clothes hanging out to dry,

RIGHT: Wherever you go in Sicily, the architecture is a feast for the eyes, packed with interest and offering tourists an enriching and enjoyable place to explore. Although it's easy to get lost, there are always shady piazzas and palm-lined squares where tourists can sit and recuperate and appreciate the loveliness that surrounds them.

PAGE 376: Even pavements are things of beauty in Sicily as this black and white patterned expanse in Piazza Nove Aprile in the hugely popular tourist town of Taormina, a town of many fourteenth and fifteenth century buildings, demonstrates.

PAGE 377: Palm trees reaching up towards the brilliantly blue sky add to the beauty of Palermo's cathedral, which reflects the varied history of the island and is a mix of Arab, Norman, and Gothic architectural influences.

CAGLIARI AND SARDINIA

CAGLIARI AND SARDINIA

The second largest island in Italy and the Mediterranean, Sardinia has turquoise seas teeming with aquatic life, arguably the best beaches in Europe, and rugged mountainous countryside. This island is the favorite holiday destination of Italians, who love the dramatic coastline, pretty fishing ports, and the exciting Sardinian nightlife. The most famous part of the island is the Costa Smeralda (the Emerald Coast), established by the Aga Khan in the 1960s and still a holiday playground for the very rich. The former Italian Prime Minister Silvio Berlusconi has not one, but three houses here, and the luxury boats moored in the marinas

speak volumes about the wealth that is attracted to this rose-hued northeast corner of the island.

Sardinia's ancient history is highly visible with more than 7,000 giant cone-shaped stone towers—the nuraghi—found all over the island and bearing testament to the nuragic people who lived here until the arrival of the Romans. These fortress-style towers were the islanders' houses, sheep shelters, and places of worship and they date back to 1700 B.C. Recent archeological excavations have unearthed a Sardinia that is even more ancient. A human skeleton from 150,000 B.C. has been discovered as have dried grape remains that have been date-tested as the oldest

grapes in the world. It is possible that Sardinia may well be the Mediterranean's original wine-growing area. Today the main agricultural activity is based on sheep rearing for wool and cheese—Sardinia's pecorino is world famous—and shepherds and their shaggy flocks can be seen all over the wild scrub-covered interior. In fact, sheep outnumber Sardinians by nearly three to one. The interior was where most people lived up until relatively recently and apart from the major ports of Cagliari, the capital in the south, and Alghero, in the northwest, few places on its coastline were heavily inhabited. This was mainly because the coastal strips were affected by malaria and it was only in 1950 that the disease was finally wiped out. Since then the Sardinians have embraced the sea, and fishing and tourism have become increasingly important industries

The attraction of Sardinia's fabulous beaches and mysterious and enchanting mountains can lead to many people being fooled. An island in the middle of a pretty big

sea leads to great extremes of climate. Summers are swelteringly hot, particularly in August, when beaches are packed with tourists and many locals have shut up shop and gone on vacation themselves. Sardinia is also prone to short but severe storms that appear without notice. It has winters that are mild but very wet and windy.

The capital, Cagliari, is a large and ancient port with a charming medieval center, bird-filled lagoons, and excellent beaches nearby. With a wonderfully preserved second century Roman amphitheater and imposing medieval twin towers —Torre di San Pancrazio and Torre dell'Elefante—the city is used by most people as their gateway to the quiet roads of the interior and the beautiful cork oak forests and for the very lucky a chance to spot the increasingly rare and diminutive native donkeys, which are now an endangered species.

PAGES 378–379: Porto Cervo is the jewel of the Costa Smeralda and is located in the gulf of the same name in northern Sardinia.

LEFT: Gesturi sits on a large plateau in the center of the island and is surrounded by some of the most interesting countryside in the whole of Sardinia. The ancient ruins of 23 Nuraghi Towers, cork woods, volcanic craters, hot springs, and a whole host of wildlife including Sardinia's almond-eyed, small but fiery, wild ponies.

LEFT: Cagliari—the capital of the island of Sardinia—viewed from the sea. There have been people living around this area since the Phoenicians first settled. They were followed by Carthaginians, Romans, Vandals, Byzantines, Pisans, Aragonese, and Austrians and before Sardinia became part of Italy.

ABOVE: Sheep outnumber Sardinians by nearly three to one. Pastures cover more than half the island allowing 2.5 million sheep—one-third of Italy's total—to roam.

BELOW: Mass in Alghero Cathedral is still conducted in an ancient tongue, that is infinitely more Spanish than Italian. The Christmas Eve Mass in the Duomo features an ancient Sibyl chant whose origin is lost in the mists of time. The cathedral's six-sided Gothic bell-tower is over 120 feet high.

RIGHT: The seventeenth-century marble-covered Roselli fountain in Sassari has water flowing from the heads of twelve lions and the statues on each corner are meant to represent the four seasons. At its peak is a statue of Saint Gavino on horseback.

ABOVE: The Tower of San Pancrazio, in Cagliari, was built in 1305 under the rule of the Pisans. Visitors can climb to the top which affords wonderful views of the whole city.

RIGHT: The soft terra-cotta colors of this Sardinian house are typical of the local architecture. The disordered arrangement of the windows probably means that they were opened up at various intervals in the building's history.

ABOVE: The fortress towers that surround the old center of Alghero were designed to be multipurpose. Primarily defensive with openings in their thick walls for canons to be able to fire from, their walls were also useful in terms of keeping people from getting out of them. Several became prisons.

RIGHT: The harbor in Alghero is now accustomed to receiving the numerous yachts and pleasure craft that cruise the Mediterranean during the summer. The hexagonal bell-tower and dome of the Duomo are visible above the harbor buildings.

PAGES 390–391: This modern church was designed by Italian jet-set architect Michele Busiri Vici in the early 1960s at Porto Cervo. Insid it boasts El Greco's *Mater Dolorosa*, a donation from the Baroness Bentink.

LEFT: The Romanesque church of Saccargia in the northern Sardinian plains, with its elaborate alternate black and white stonework, looks like it should be sitting in Tuscany. Built in A.D. 1114 the design of the church follows the Pisan and Luccan architectural models but with its thirteenth-century frescoes and unique setting this extraordinary church is very much a one off.

ABOVE: The interior of Sardinia is little visited but huge rewards await those who go inland. There are estimated to be 7,000 to 8,000 "nuraghi" scattered throughout the island. These cut-off cone-shaped stone towers are remnants of the nuragic people who built them as fortresses and as habitations and shelters for animals. Some date from as far back as 3500 B.C.

LEFT: Sardinia is only 160 miles long and around 75 miles across and is filled with charming examples of the old Sardinia, before people moved to the coastal areas to find work. Old villages with tiny churches and thousands of sheep and their careful shepherds inhabit the central areas.

PAGE 396: Sassari's Duomo di San Nicola di Bari is a fifteenth century cathedral with Baroque touches and this fine Campanile.

PAGE 397: The square bell tower next to the Duomo of Cagliari is from the original building that was constructed by the Pisans in the thirteenth century. The 1933 neo-Roman façade replaced an early eighteenth century Baroque front. Inside is the original pulpit designed by Guglielmo da Pisa in 1160 and donated to the cathedral in 1312.

PAGE 398: The pink hued Costa Smeralda on the north-eastern corner of Sardinia was built by the Aga Khan in the 1960s and is the most fashionable and expensive place to visit on the island.

PAGE 399: Sardinia is one of the most unspoilt and romantic islands of the Mediterranean. The ports and major resorts are overwhelmed in the summer, particularly August, but there are still places off the beaten track to be discovered and enjoyed in tranquillity.

Photo Credits

Arcaid: 16, 75B

Colin Dixon/Arcaid.co.uk: 104–107, 114–117,
120–122, 132–133, 154–155, 159–161, 169, 235
Ian Lambot/Arcaid.co.uk: 62–63, 68, 69, 90–92, 94,
96–97, 138–139, 147, 152–153
Joe Cornish/Arcaid.co.uk: 4, 14–15, 17–19, 21–25,
28, 30–31, 36–60, 64, 70–74, 88, 98–99, 102–103,
108–113, 123, 124, 126–131, 136–137, 140–146,
148–151, 156–158, 162, 163, 193, 210–220,
222–224, 226–234, 236–237, 239–244, 246–255,
351, 352, 362, 363, 366, 400
Richard Bryant/Arcaid.co.uk: 61, 65–67, 75T,
76–77, 93, 118, 119, 125
Robert O'Dea/Arcaid.co.uk: 134–135
Valeria Carullo/ Arcaid.co.uk: 320–321, 324, 325,
328–329, 330B, 331–337, 340–344

Corbis: 164

Bob Krist/Corbis: 12, 29, 302–304
Danny Lehman/Corbis: 318
David Sailors/Corbis: 316–317
Giraud Philippe/Corbis Sygma: 383, 387, 399
John and Lisa Merrill/Corbis: 311, 313
John Heseltine/Corbis: 393
Jose Fuste Raga/Corbis: 32

Ladislav Janicek/zefa/Corbis: 382, 389, 392
Marco Cristofori/Corbis: 300–301
Mimmo Jodice/Corbis: 312
Owen Franken/Corbis: 296–297
P.J.Sharpe/zefa/Corbis: 305
Richard T. Nowitz/Corbis: 309
Roger Ressmeyer/Corbis: 310
Sandro Vannini/Corbis: 262–263, 314–315, 394–395
Stefan Schuetz/zefa/Corbis: 260–261
Vince Steano/Corbis: 319
Wolfgang Deuter/zefa/Corbis: 289T

David Lyons: 348–349, 364–365, 367–369

Getty Images: 20, 176–177, 330T, 346T, 346B, 347B
Altrendo/Getty Images: 190–191
Dorling Kindersley/Getty Images: 11
Iconica/Getty Images: 206, 208–209
Laura Ronchi/Getty Images: 166–167, 170–171,
174–175, 181, 184–185, 268, 269T, 273, 276T,
286, 326–327, 338, 339, 345, 376
Lonely Planet/Getty Images: 10, 172, 180, 372–375,
380–381
National Geographic/Getty Images: 33, 196–197,
298–299, 306–308, 322–323
Neil Beer/Getty Images: 95
Panoramic Images/Getty Images: 278–279

Photographer's Choice/Getty Images: 201, 204–205,
370–371
Robert Harding World Imagery/Getty Images: 2–3,
6–7, 13, 178–179, 182–183, 186–187, 202–203,
207, 221, 270–271, 277, 280–281, 284, 291, 292,
294, 295, 377–379, 390–391, 398
Stone/Getty Images: 34–35, 173, 192, 225,
258–259, 264–265
The Image Bank/Getty Images: 8–9, 26–27, 168,
188–189, 256–257, 272B, 274–275, 290, 354–355

Italian Tourist Board
Fototeca ENIT/Paola Ghirotti: 194, 282
Fototeca ENIT/Vito Arcomano: 1, 195, 198–200,
238, 245 both, 266–267, 269B, 272T, 276B, 283,
285, 287, 288, 289B, 293, 384–386, 388, 396, 397

Hugh Alexander 78, 79, 82–87, 100–101, 165
both, 350, 353, 356–359, 360–361

BELOW: With its ancient ports, outstanding coast
and wild interior with its ancient history, Sardinia
is a true island of contrasts. The main cities of
Cagliari and Alghero offer busy sea port life and
cafes and bars, but drive just 30 minutes inland
and there is another more ancient and mysterious
world.